The Human Voice

THE HUMAN VOICE.

WORKS BY THE SAME AUTHOR.

HYDROPATHIC ENCYCLOPEDIA,	$4 40	ALCOHOLIC CONTROVERSY,	50
THE HYGIENIC HAND BOOK,	2 00	WATER CURE for the MILLION,	30
SEXUAL PHYSIOLOGY,	2 00	TRUE HEALING ART,	30 or 50
UTERINE DISPLACEMENTS,		HYDROPATHIC COOK BOOK,	$1 50
COLORED PLATES,	5 00	FAMILY GYMNASIUM,	1 50
THROAT AND LUNGS,	25	HOME TREAT. SEX. ABUSE,	50
DIGESTION AND DYSPEPSIA,	1 00	THE BATH—Its Uses,	25 or 50
MOTHER'S HYGIENIC HAND-BOOK,	1 00	HYGEIAN HOME COOK BOOK,	25
		HYGIENIC CATECHISM,	10

A Set of Six Anatomical and Physiological Plates, $20.

THE

HUMAN VOICE:

ITS ANATOMY, PHYSIOLOGY, PATHOLOGY,
THERAPEUTICS, AND TRAINING;

WITH

RULES OF ORDER FOR LYCEUMS.

BY

R. T. TRALL, M.D.,

PRINCIPAL AND FOUNDER OF THE HYGEIO-THERAPEUTIC COLLEGE; PROFESSOR
OF INSTITUTES OF MEDICINE, AND AUTHOR OF NUMEROUS WORKS.

NEW YORK:
S. R. WELLS & COMPANY.
737 BROADWAY.
1875.

PREFACE.

THE object of this little work is to present, in a cheap and convenient form, the facts and principles applicable to the culture and uses of the Human Voice, which are only to be found scattered through several large volumes, and to furnish Lyceums and Debating Clubs with a concise Code of Rules and Usages for the regulation of their proceedings. It is not expected nor intended to supersede the more elaborate works on Elocution, which may be indispensable for the Orator and Teacher; but to furnish all who desire to read and speak well, and who must rely mainly on self-education, with a plain and intelligible guide in theory and practice.

R. T. T.

FLORENCE HIGHTS, N. J., 1875.

CONTENTS.

CONTENTS.

CHAPTER V.—TRAINING OF THE VOICE.

CHAPTER VI.—EXERCISES ON THE ELEMENTARY SOUNDS.

CHAPTER VII.—SELECTIONS FOR PRACTICE.

THE HUMAN VOICE.

CHAPTER I.

ANATOMY OF THE VOICE.

THE special apparatus of the voice is the larynx, an arrangement of ligaments and muscles at the upper part of the windpipe (trachea). The quality of voice depends on the tension and approximation of the vocal cords; its depth or fullness depends on the capacity of the chest, and its power on the associated action of all the respiratory muscles. A brief exposition, therefore, of the structure of the vocal and respiratory apparatus seems to be necessary as a basis for the intelligent training and proper exercise of the organs of music and speech.

The foundation for a normal voice as well as for bodily and mental vigor, and, indeed, for good health, is a well-developed thorax, or framework of the chest.

This is constituted of the sternum, or breast-bone, in front, and the twelve pairs of ribs on the sides. The ribs are articulated behind with the twelve dorsal vertebræ of the spinal column. The trachea commences opposite the fifth cerrical vertebræ, and extends to the third dorsal, where it divides into the right and left bronchi, which pass to the right and left lung, and are subdivided and ramified throughout the substance of the lungs. The trachea and bronchial tubes are everywhere lined with a mucous membrane, as is the mouth and larynx. Two-thirds of the anterior cylinder of the

Fig. 1.

THE THORAX.

An anterior view of the thorax is represented in Fig. 1. 1. The manubrium. 2. Body. 3. Ensiform cartilage. 4. First dorsal vertebra. 5. Last dorsal vertebra. 6. First rib. 7. Head of first rib. 8. Its neck. 9. Its tubercle. 10. Seventh rib. 11. Costal cartilages of the ribs. 12. Last two false ribs. 13. The groove along the lower border of each rib.

trachea are composed of fifteen to twenty cartilaginous rings, which are conducive to the vibrations of air in making trilling sounds.

The thyroid gland (sometimes the seat of goitre, or bronchocele,) is situated upon the trachea above the sternum; it is divided into two lobes, one of which is placed on each side of the trachea.

The lungs occupy the cavity of the chest on each side of the heart. They are conical in shape, tapering above, where they extend beyond the level of the first rib, and broad and concave below, where they rest on the convex surface of the diaphragm. The root or upper portion of

Fig. 2.

HEART AND LUNGS.

Fig. 2 represents the anterior aspect of the anatomy of the heart and lungs. 1. Right ventricle ; the vessels to the left of the number are the middle coronary artery and veins. 2. Left ventricle. 3. Right auricle. 4. Left auricle. 5. Pulmonary artery. 6. Right pulmonary artery. 7. Left pulmonary artery. 8. Remains of the ductus arteriosus. 9. Aortic arch. 10. Superior cava. 11. Arteria innominata; in front of it is the right vena innominata. 12, Right subclavian vein ; behind it is its corresponding artery. 13. Right common carotid artery and vein. 14. Left vena innominata. 15, Left carotid artery and vein. 16. Left subclavian artery and vein. 17. Trachea. 18. Right bronchus. 19. Left bronchus. 20, 20. Pulmonary veins; 18, 20, from the root of the right lung; and 7, 19, 20, the root of the left. 21. Upper lobe of the right lung. 22. Its middle lobe. 23. Its inferior lobe. 24 Superior lobe of left lung. 25. Its lower lobe.

each lung, which retains the organ in position, comprises the pulmonary artery and veins, the bronchial tubes, the bronchial vessels, and the pulmonary plexuses of nerves.

The minute anatomy of the larynx is shown in figs. 3 and 4.

Fig. 3.

Fig. 3 is a vertical section of the larynx, showing its ligaments. 1. Body of the os hyoides. 2. Its great cornu. 3. Its lesser cornu. 4. The ala of the thyroid. 5. The superior cornu. 6. Its inferior cornu. 7. Promum Adami. 8, 8. Thyro-hyoidean membrane; the opening near the posterior numeral transmits the superior laryngeal nerve and artery. 9. Thyro-hyoidean ligament. *a.* Epiglottis. *b.* Hypo-epiglottic ligament. *c.* Thyro-epiglottic. *d.* Arytenoid cartilage. *e.* Outer angle of its base. *f.* Corniculum laryngis. *g.* Cuneiform cartilage. *h.* Superior thyro-arytenoid ligament. *i.* Chorda vocalis, or inferior thyro-arytenoid; the elliptical space between the two thyro-arytenoid; is the laryngeal ventricle. *k.* Cricoid cartilage. *l.* Lateral portion of the crico-thyroidean membrane. *m.* Its central portion. *n.* Upper ring of the trachea, which is received within the ring of the cricoid cartilage. *o.* Section of the isthmus of the thyroid gland. *p, p.* The levator of the glandulæ thyroideæ.

LIGAMENTS OF THE LARYNX.

Fig. 4.

Fig. 4 is a side view of the larynx, one ala of the thyroid cartilage being removed. 1. Remaining ala. 2. One of the arytenoid cartilages. 3. One of the cornicula laryngis. 4. Cricoid cartilage. 5. Posterior crico-arytenoid muscle. 6. Crico-arytenoideus lateralis. 7. Thyro-arytenoideus. 8. Crico-thyroidean membrane. 9. One half of the epiglottis. 10. Upper part of the trachea.

The following description of the laryngeal structures is copied from the "Hydropathic Encylopædia:

THE LARYNX LATERALLY.

"The cartilages are : 1. *Thyroid* (shield-like), which consists of two lateral portions (*alæ*) meeting at an angle in front, and forming the projecting part of the throat, called *pomum Adami* (Adam's apple). Each ala forms a rounded border posteriorly, which terminates above in a *superior cornu*, and below in an *inferior cornu*. 2. *Cricoid* (like a ring), a circular ring, narrow in front and broad behind, where it has two rounded surfaces, which articulate with the arytenoid cartilages. The œsophagus is attached to a vertical ridge on its posterior surface. 3. Two *arytenoid* (pitcher-like); triangular in form, and broad and thick below, where they articulate with the upper border of the cricoid; above they are pointed and prolonged by two small pyriform cartilages, called *cornicula laryngis*, which form part of the lateral wall of the larynx, and afford attachment to the chorda vocalis and several of the articulatiug muscles. 4. Two *cuneiform*; small cylinders, about seven lines in length, and enlarged at each extremity; they are attached by the lower end to the arytenoid, and their upper extremity forms a prominence on the border of the arytenoepiglottidean fold of membrane; they are occasionally wanting. 5. *Epiglottis*; shaped like a cordate leaf, and situated immediately in front of the opening of the larynx, which it closes when the larynx is drawn up beneath the base of the tongue, as in the act of swallowing. The laryngeal cartilages ossify more or less in old age, particularly in the male.

"The *ligaments* are: 1. Three *thyro-hyoidean*, which connect the thyroid cartilage with the os hyoides. 2. Two *capsular crico-thyroid*, which articulate the thyroid with the cricoid, and with their synovial membranes from the articulation between the inferior cornu and sides of the cricoid. 3. The *crico-thyroidean membrane*, a fan-shaped layer of elastic tissue, attached by its apex to the lower border of the thyroid, and by its expanded margin to the upper border of the cricoid and base of the arytenoid; above it is continuous with the lower margin of the chorda vocalis. 4. Two *capsular crico-arytenoid*, which connect those cartilages. 5. Two *superior thyro-arytenoid*, thin bands between the receding angle of the thyroid and the anterior inner border of each arytenoid; the lower border constituting the upper boundary of the ventricle of the larynx. 6. Two *inferior thyro-arytenoid*, the *chordæ vocales*, which are thicker than the superior, and, like them, composed of elastic tissue. Each ligament, or vocal chord, is attached in front to the receding angle of the thyroid, and behind to the anterior angle of the base of the arytenoid. The inferior border of the chorda vocalis is continuous with the lateral expansion of the crico-thyroid ligament. The superior border forms the lower boundary of the ventricle of the larynx. The space between the two chordæ vocales is the *glottis* or *rima glottidis*. 7. Three *glosso-epiglottic*, folds of mucous membrane connecting the anterior surface of the epiglottis with the root of the tongue. 8. The *hyo-epiglottic*, an elastic band connecting the anterior aspect of the epiglottis with the hyoid bone. 9. The *thryo-epiglottic*, a slender elastic slip embracing the apex of the epiglottis, and inserted into the thyroid above the chordæ vocalæs.

"The *muscles* are eight in number: five larger ones of the chordæ vocales and glottis, and three smaller of the epiglottis. The origin, insertion, and use of each is expressed by its name. They are the *crico-thyroid*, *posterior* and *lateral crico-arytenoid*, *thyro-arytenoid*, *arytenoid thyro-epiglottic*, and *superior* and *inferior aryteno-epiglottic*. The posterior crico-arytenoid opens the glottis; the arytenoid approximates the arytenoid cartilages posteriorly, and the crico-arytenoideus lateralis and thyro-arytenoidei anteriorly; the latter also close the glottis mesially. The crico-thyroidei are tensors of the vocal chords, and with the thyro-arytenoidei, regulate their position and vibrating length. The remaining muscles assist in regulating the tension of the vocal chords by varying the position of their cartilages.

"The *aperture* of the larynx is a triangular opening, broad in front and narrow behind; bounded in front by the epiglottis, behind by the arytenoid muscle, and on the sides by the folds of the mucous membrane. The cavity is divided into two parts by an oblong constriction produced by the prominence of the vocal chords; the part above the constriction is broad above and narrow below, and the part beneath is narrow above and broad below, while the space included by the constriction is a narrow, triangular fissure, the *glottis*, bounded on the sides by the chordæ vocales and inner surface of the arytenoid cartilages, and behind by the arytenoid muscle; it is nearly an inch in length, somewhat longer in the male than female. Immediately above the prominence caused by the chorda vocalis, and extending nearly its length on each side of the cavity of the larynx is the *ventricle of the larynx*, an elliptical fossa which serves to isolate the chord.

"The *mucous membrane* lines the entire cavity of the larynx, its prominences and depressions, and is continuous with that of the mouth and pharynx, which is prolonged through the trachea and bronchial tubes into the lungs. In the ventricles of the larynx the membrane forms a cæcal pouch, called *sacculus laryngis*, on the surface of which are the openings of numerous follicular glands, whose secretion lubricates the vocal chords."

The abdominal muscles are important parts of the respiratory machinery; comparing the lungs to a bellows, these muscles constitute the handles, and unless they are well developed and in vigorous condition, the voice be correspondingly feeble and imperfect. The relation of these muscles to the thorax directly, and to the lungs and vocal apparatus indirectly, is shown in figs. 5 and 6.

Fig. 5.

MUSCLES OF THE TRUNK.

In Fig. 5 are seen the muscles of the trunk anteriorly. The superficial layer is seen on the left side. and the deeper on the right. 1, Pectoralis major. 2. Deltoid. 3. Anterior border of the latissimus dorsi. 4. Serrations of the serratus magnus. 5. Subclavius of the right side. 6. Pectoralis minor. 7. Coracho-brachialis. 8. Upper part of the biceps, showing its two heads. 9. Coracoid process of the scapula. 10. Serratus magnus of the right side. 11. External intercostal. 12. External oblique. 13. Its aponeurosis; the median line to the right of this number is the linea alba; the flexuous line to the left is the linea semilunaris; the transverse lines above and below the number are the lineæ transversæ. 14. Poupart's ligament. 15. External abdominal ring; the margin above is called the *superior* or *internal* pillar; the margin below the *inferior* or *external* pillar; the curved intercolumnar fibres are seen proceeding upward from Poupart's ligament to strengthen the ring. The numbers 14 and 15 are situated upon the fascia lata of the thigh; the opening to the right of 15 is called *saphenous*. 16. Rectus of the right side. 17. Pyramidalis. 18. Internal oblique. 19. The common tendon of the internal oblique and transversalis descending behind Poupart's ligament to the pectineal line. 20. The arch formed between the lower curved border of the internal oblique and Poupart's ligament beneath which the spermatic cord passes, and hernia occurs.

Fig. 6 is a side view of the muscles of the trunk. 1. Costal region of the latissimus dorsi. 2. Serratus magnus. 3. Upper part of external oblique. 4. Two external intercostals. 5. Two internal intercostals. 6. Transversalis. 7. Its posterior aponeurosis. 8. Its anterior. 9. Lower part of the left rectus. 10. Right rectus. 11. The arched opening where the spermatic cord passes and hernia takes place. 12. The gluteus maximus, and medius, and tensor vaginæ femoris muscles invested by fascia lata.

Fig. 6.

MUSCLES OF THE TRUNK LATERALLY.

The oblique muscles flex the thorax on the pelvis; either acting singly, twists the body to one side. Either transversalis muscle by contracting diminishes the size of the abdomen, and both acting together constrict its general cavity. The recti muscles, and the pyramidalis pull the thorax forward when acting together.

All of the abdominal muscles are auxiliary to respiration, and as they constitute the chief forces in expelling the air from the lungs, their relation to voice is obvious. As respiratory muscles they are aided by the muscles of the loins and back; the united action of all these muscles compresses the abdomen in all directions, as may be noticed in prolonged coughing or severe vomiting.

CHAPTER II.

Fig. 7.

NATURAL SPINE.

PHYSICAL uprightness is as important for a public speaker as moral rectitude is for a private citizen. Other things being equal, every person will have a power to please and persuade, influence and direct the minds of others, through the media of speech and music, measurable generally by the integrity of the whole bodily organization, and especially by the erectitude of the spinal column (Fig. 7), without which the extensive and complicated machinery of respiration and vocalization cannot act harmoniously.

The vocal apparatus has been compared to a stringed, tubular, and reeded instrument, as the violin, flute, and clarionet; it has many properties in common with each, and, indeed, with all musical instruments; yet it differs in many respects from either. No mechanical contrivance can rival the variety and delicacy of action of the living structure, hence the human voice must ever be incomparably superior, as a musical instrument, to all human inventions. A good reader, a good speaker, or a good singer never fails to attract the multitudes.

The lower vocal cords are chiefly instrumental in the production of *sound*. If the upper cords are removed, voice continues, but is rendered feeble; if the lower cords are destroyed, voice is entirely lost.

The *tones of voice* depend on the varying tension of the vocal cords. In producing tones, the ligaments of opposite sides are brought into approaching parallelism with each other, by the approximation of the points of the arytenoid cartilages; in the intervals they are again separated, and the opening between them, termed *rima glottidis*, assumes the form of the letter V, as represented in Fig. 8.

Fig. 8 exhibits the vocal ligaments as seen superiorly. G, E, H. Thyroid cartilage. N, F. Arytenoid cartilages. S, V, S, V. Vocal cords or ligaments. N, X. Crico-arytenoideus lateralis. V, k, f. Right thyro-arytenoideus. N, l, N, l. Crico-arytenoidei postici. B, B. Crico-arytenoid ligament.

Fig. 8.

LARYNX FROM ABOVE.

The muscles which stretch or relax the vocal ligaments, are alone directly concerned in the voice; the muscles which open and close the glottis, regulate the amount of the air inspired and expired.

The *pitch of the tones* is regulated by the tension of the vocal cords; its *volume* or intensity depends on the capacity of the lungs, length of the trachea, flexibility of

the vocal cords, and the force with which the air is expelled from the lungs. The *character* of the voice is
dependent on the confirmation of the pharynx, mouth, and
nasal cavities. In the male the larynx is more prominent
and the vocal cords are longer than in the female, in the
proportion of three to two, which renders the voice in
most cases an octave lower.

The free play of the diaphragm is an important factor
in the volume of voice. To understand this matter fully
it must be recollected that the movements of the respira
tory apparatus are partly voluntary, for the purposes of
being subservient to voice and speech, and partly invol-
untary, for the purposes of aerating the blood. The lungs
themselves are entirely passive in respiration. When the
walls of the chest are drawn asunder, and the thorax
dilated by the action of the respiratory muscles, the at-
mospheric air rushes into the air-cells, distending them
in proportion to the dilatation of the thorax, and keeping
the surface of the lungs accurately in contact with the
walls of the chest in all their movements. But if air be
admitted into the cavity of the pleura, outside of the
lungs, as by a penetrating wound, the lungs cannot be
fully distended by inspiration, but will remain partially
collapsed, although the thorax expands, for the reason
that the pressure from without balances that within the
air-cells. Fig. 9 illustrates the action of the diaphragm
in respiration.

The diaphragm, by extending the ribs and pressing
down the abdominal viscera, is the principal agent in inspiration. In a deep inspiration, the little muscles between the ribs (intercostals) assist in the expansion of
the chest by spreading the ribs, aided also to some extent by the muscles of the thorax generally. Expiration,

as already stated, is mainly accomplished by the contraction of the abdominal muscles, which, by drawing down the ribs and compressing the viscera up against the relaxed diaphragm, diminish the cavity of the thorax from above.

Says Marshall (*Outlines of Physiology*): "The human vocal apparatus is analogous to a wind instrument with a double membranous tongue, the bronchi and trachea representing the wind-tube, the vocal cords the double

Fig 9.

ACTION OF THE DIAPHRAGM.

Fig. 9 is a side view of the chest and abdomen in respiration. 1. Cavity of the chest. 2. Cavity of the abdomen. 3. Line of direction for the diaphragm when relaxed in expiration. 4. Line of direction when contracted in inspiration. 5, 6. Position of the front walls of the chest and abdomen in inspiration. 7, 8. Their position in expiration.

membranous tongue, and the parts above the glottis the attached tube. For the production of vocal sounds, even the feeblest, more air must pass through the glottis than in respiration; and this current of air must undergo periodic interruptions in its passage through that fissure. The vocal cords, moreover, are made more or less tense, and are approximated so as to be parallel to each other, and the fissure of the glottis is converted into a fine chink-like opening. The escape of the air propelled upward through the trachea being thus retarded, the margins of the vocal cords are forced upward, and slightly separated from each other; the elasticity of the cords is now called into play, so that they counteract the force of the impulse communicated to them, and, by a downward recoiling movement, again narrow the glottis. In this manner, the oscillations into which the vocal cords are thrown by the escape of the air driven from the trachea, or wind-tube, are communicated to the less tense air above the glottis, and throw this into vibrations. By means of the laryngeal ventricles, or sacs, placed above the vocal cords, these latter are kept free, so that their vibrations are easily accomplished. It has also been supposed by some, that the superior vocal cords maintain the strength and quality of the sounds, by entering into simultaneous and synchronous vibrations. This is contrary to Señor Garcia's observations with the laryngoscope; but he found that, in elevation of the pitch of the voice, whether natural or falsetto, the superior vocal cords approached each other, so as to narrow the part of the vocal tube above the glottis."

The ordinary range of the human voice, from the lowest male to the highest female voice, is nearly 4 octaves.

Fig. 10. E.

Fig. 11. C.

Fig. 12. F.

Fig. 13. A.

The lowest note, E (Fig. 10), is caused by 80 vibrations per second, and the highest note, C (Fig. 11), by 1,024 vibrations per second. But in exceptional cases, the range may be nearly 5½ octaves, the lowest note, F (Fig. 12), being caused by 42; and the highest note, A (Fig. 13), by 1,708 vibrations.

In ordinary speech, the range of voice is usually about half an octave; but in singing, the compass of the voice in the same individual generally extends over 2 octaves. In rare cases it has extended over 3½ octaves. It has been calculated that no less than 240 different states of tension of the vocal cords are producible at will, each degree of tension modifying the sound of the note in singing, or of the tone in speaking, and all this in a voice of ordinary range. Celebrated singers can produce a still greater number of intermediate tones. "Madame Mara," says Marshall, "could effect as many as 2,000 changes."

The bass and tenor varieties of voice are characteristic of the male, and the contralto and the soprano, otherwise known as second treble and first treble, of the female sex. The subdivision of voice called baritone, is intermediate between the tenor and bass, and the mezzo-soprano is intermediate between the soprano and contralto. The lowest note of the contralto is about an octave higher than the lowest note of the bass voice; and the highest soprano about an octave higher than the highest tenor.

The personal quality or peculiar tone of voice is due to the general confirmation of the air-passages; but in both sexes, more especially in the male, two series of notes can be produced, which have been distinguished into the true or chest notes, and the falsetto or head notes. The chest notes are called those of the natural voice, and are fuller, stronger, and more resonant, and are the lower notes of the voice; the falsetto notes are softer, less clear, and have a humming sound resembling the harmonic notes of strings. The middle notes of the scale can be produced by either the chest or the head voice. Some persons can speak or sing with either voice so well marked as to seem to be endowed with two distinct voices. Various theories have been advanced to account for the falsetto voice; but the observations of Garcia seem to prove that, during the production of the falsetto notes, the glottis is more elongated and widened, and that only the edges of the vocal cords are approximated, thus offering little resistance to the air, whilst, in the natural or chest voice, a certain depth of the surface of each cord is made to approach the other, and to undergo vibrations.

In certain strong mental emotions, the muscles of the voice act spasmodically, as in sobbing and laughter, and sometimes closing the glottis entirely for a longer or shorter time, as in some convulsive diseases.

Speech is the utterance of articulate sounds. The voice or vowel sounds are made with a nearly fixed position of the vocal organs; but as those sounds are modified by the action of the tongue, lips, etc., they are called articulate or consonant sounds. The vowel sounds are specially expressive of the feelings, while the consonant sounds are specially related to thought. This is why the language of music is so largely constituted of vowel sounds, the difference between music and speech consisting simply in the prolongation of the vowel sounds. As the language of all animals expresses much more of the affectional than of the intellectual mind, they have correspondingly little occasion for consonant sounds.

As vocalization depends on laryngeal vibrations, in whispering, vowels are articulated simply by the action of the mouth and fauces, all sound being produced above the larynx. Sighing is another example of sound produced above the larynx; if the vocal cords are called into vibratory action, the sigh becomes a groan. Most of the letters of the alphabet can be articulated with very little laryngeal action during inspiration.

Many sounds, as of smacking, clicking, kissing, and whistling, are generated in the mouth, and produced independently of laryngeal action.

Ventriloquism consists essentially in the imitation of

peculiar sounds. Its rationale is not well understood by physiologists. Magendie supposed it to be produced in the larynx. Some have thought it was produced simply by articulating while drawing in the breath. According to Muller, the sounds peculiar to ventriloquism may be made, after taking a deep inspiration, so as to occasion the protrusion of the abdominal viscera by the descent of the diaphragm, and maintaining the diaphragm in its depressed or contracted condition, by speaking during a very slow expiration, performed only by the lateral parieties of the chest, through a very narrow glottis.

Speaking automata have only succeeded in imitating the separate sounds of the voice; they can never combine them successfully so as to imitate the language of the vital organism.

The following lucid explanation of the various vowal and consonant sounds is copied from "Marshall's Physiology:"

"Articulate sounds are divided into vowels and consonants. The true *vowels*, or *open sounds*, as they are called, are generated in the larynx. They are merely uninterrupted vocal tones, variously modified in their outward passage, by alterations in the shape of the parts of the oral cavity through which they pass; thus, in uttering the pure vowel sounds, $\bar{a}$, $\breve{a}$, e, o, u, pronounced respectively as in the words far, fate, ell, old, and in French words containing the u, one and the same sound produced by the vibrations of the vocal cords is converted into five different sounds, by changes in the position of the tongue, and by the gradual prolongation of the cavity of the mouth, by means of the lips; the most natural of these vowel sounds, or the one most easily uttered, is the broad $\bar{a}$. In the same manner the *diphthong* sound, i, ei, eu,

2

and the sounds of *y* and *w*, at the beginning of words are vocal tones, modified by further changes in the shape and form of the mouth.

"*Consonants*, or *shut sounds*, are entirely formed in the parts above the larynx, and are so named, because most, if not all of them, can only be sounded *consonantly*, that is, with another sound or vowel. They require, for their production, a shutting or valve-like action to take place, either between the lips, as in pronouncing the letters *b, p,* and *m ;* or between the upper teeth and lower lip, as in the case of *f* and *v ;* or between the tongue and the palate, as *d, g* hard, *c* hard, *k, q, t, r, l,* and *n,* or between the tongue and the teeth, as in the production of hissing sounds, such as *c* soft, or *s* and *z.* The *compound articulate sounds,* as *j,* or *g* soft, *ch* soft, *ch* guttural, *ph, sh, th, ng* and *x,* are produced by modifications, or combinations of some of the other pure consonant sounds. The aspirate *h* is produced by an increased expiratory effort, made with the mouth open, before a vowel or other sound.

"Those consonants which are produced by, or connected with, a sudden stoppage of the breath at a certain point, the opening leading from the pharynx to the nose being quite closed, and all the respired air passing through the mouth, are called *explosive* consonants. They are of two kinds: the simple explosive consonants, *b, d,* and *g* hard ; and the aspirate explosives, *p, t, k ;* these, when uttered, are unaccompanied by a vocal sound, that is, they are attended with an intonation of the voice. Those consonants which can be produced without a complete stoppage of the breath previous to their utterance, are called *continuous ;* some of these sounds are developed by the passage of the air, with a degree of friction through the mouth; in this way the consonants *v*, *f*, *s*, and *z*, are produced by expiration through the nose only, as *ng*, *m*, and *n*. In uttering the letters *l* and *r*, the air escapes through the nose and mouth; in pronouncing the first of these, the air escapes at the sides of the tongue; in pronouncing the sound, the tongue undergoes a vibrating movement. All the continuous consonants can be pronounced with a vocal sound, except the aspirate *h;* and some of them can be pronounced either with or without vocal intonation. Consonants have also been named according to the seat of their production; thus *p* is called a *labial*, *t* a *palatal*, *n* a *nasal*, and the Gaelic *ch* a *guttural* consonant; but this classification is exceedingly artificial and incorrect; for the greater number of articulate sounds are the result of the conjoined action of the mouth, lips, palate, and upper part of the air-passage."

CHAPTER III.

Fig. 14.

SPINAL MISCURVATURE.

THE most common causes of imperfect respiration and defective voice are distortions of the spinal column, and contracted chests. No person with either deformity can have a powerful voice, whatever may be its other qualities. Fig. 14, SPINAL MISCURVATURE, is a representation of a very common form of spinal distortion, in which nearly all of the abdominal viscera are more or less displaced, and the respiratory muscles unbalanced and undeveloped. By contrasting this figure with that of the natural spine in the preceding chapter (fig. 6), the disastrous consequences of a crooked spinal column may be realized at a glance.

A single glance at the bones of the chest (fig. 1), is sufficient to show the injurious effects on the respiratory system directly, and the vocal organs indirectly of every thing that interferes in the least with the full expansion of the lungs in breathing; and the relation of the diaphragm to respiration (fig. 9), explains the horrid consequences of tight-lacing. That this subject may be

(28)

fully comprehended, let us place the normal development of this vital part of the human being in contrast with the abominably abnormal condition so common in the society of fashionable American women.

Fig. 15.   Fig. 16.   Fig. 17.   Fig. 18.

NATURAL WAIST. NATURAL THORAX. CONTRACTED WAIST. FASHIONABLE WAIST.

A sufficient commentary on this fashionable folly and pernicious vice, so far as the immediate objects of this work are concerned, is the simple statement of the fact, that no female who deforms her body with tight-lacing ever becomes distinguished as a reader, speaker, or actor,

Fig. 19.

CORRECT POSITION IN STUDY.

Fig. 20.

MISPOSITION IN STUDY.

although a majority of them have attained distinction as
chronic invalids and the mothers of feeble offspring.

All crooked bodily positions, by unbalancing the whole
muscular system, enfeeble the breathing apparatus and
impair the voice. Malpositions and spinal distortions are
often acquired in the primary schools, because of the
unanatomical construction of the miserable benches on
which the suffering scholars are educated to "sit still"
several hours each day. Figs. 19 and 20 illustrate this
subject.

The malposition acquired in the sitting posture in

Fig. 21.

STANDING ERECT.

Fig. 22.

MALPOSITION IN STANDING.

childhood, is manifested in the standing posture in adult life, as represented in fig. 22, contrasted with the perpendicular position, fig. 21.

Although these deformities, which are almost always acquired in early life, can never be entirely overcome, much benefit may be derived from a persistent course of vocal culture, in connection with a proper system of gymnastic exercises; and if the laryngeal structures are favorably organized, such persons may become reputable speakers.

The habit of *sleeping with the mouth open* in early life, and especially in infancy, has a very injurious effect on the breathing and vocal organs; and not only this, but it tends to distort the jaw-bones and deform the teeth. Parents and nurses should be very careful to check this habit in its incipiency, or the damage may become irremediable. The imperfections of speech termed *lisping* and *stammering* are not attributable to organic defects, but to errors of action of the vocal apparatus. In lisping the tongue cleaves to the roof of the mouth, or is pushed against the upper teeth; stammering is occasioned by a spasmodic action of the glottis, tongue, or lips, which is always aggravated by any mental apprehension or embarrassment.

Hoarseness of voice is usually occasioned by a swelling or congestion of the mucous membrane which lines the mouth, nose, trachea, or bronchial tubes. When the laryngeal portion of the mucous membrane is extremely congested, voice is entirely lost, as happens in some cases of quinsy, diphtheria, and croup, and in the later stage of laryngeal consumption. A chronic thickening of the mucous membrane of the laryngeal sacs or ventricles sometimes occasions permanent hoarseness, or complete loss of voice. Paralysis of any one or more of the muscles of articulation may cause defect or loss of voice.

A common cause of defective voice, and sometimes of complete aphonia, is a want of association or co-operation in the action of the abdominal muscles and diaphragm in vocalization—a condition which may be occasioned by bodily malpositions, disease, or an improper use of the respiratory and vocal organs.

The *nasal tone* of voice is due to an approximation of the arches of the palate, more than to a closure of the nostrils.

The *vailed tone* of voice is occasioned by lowering the larynx so that it is covered by the entire pharynx, the base of the tongue being approximated to the palate, and the voice resounding in the upper part of the pharynx beneath the skull.

The *explosive voice*, which is due to the respired air being all passed out at the mouth, is always aggravated by a feeble co-operation of the abdominal muscles with the vocal effort. In this case the speaker becomes hoarse with any prolonged vocal effort. The explosive voice, though harsh and loud, is never heard at a great distance.

CHAPTER IV.

THERAPEUTICS OF THE VOICE.

PREMISING that, in all conditions of infirmity or disease affecting the voice, the general health is the first of all things to be attended to, this chapter will be devoted to such exercises and remedies as are specially applicable to defects of the vocal apparatus. In all cases it is important to harmonize as much as possible the action of all the muscles directly or indirectly concerned in respiration and voice; and just to the extent that this is accomplished will the disabilities or deformities be remedied, weak muscles and organs invigorated, obstructions removed, congestions reduced, and vocalization improved.

One of the best exercises is rapid walking over an uneven surface, or up and down stairs, keeping the mouth shut. The exercise should be commenced with moderation, and gradually increased in rapidity as can be borne without panting or difficulty of breathing. Those who are dyspeptic can improve the effect of this exercise by slapping the abdominal muscles as recommended in the author's work on "Digestion and Dyspepsia."

Among the "modern improvements" introduced into many health institutions, more or less useful for our purposes, are the health-lift, vibrator, dumb-bells, wands, rings, clubs, and other apparatus and machinery, each having special adaptation to some one or more of the many

abnormal conditions prevalent. But for the benefit of
those who are obliged to depend on self-treatment, a few
illustrations, specially adapted to the respiratory and vocal
apparatus, are copied from the author's "Illustrated
Family Gymnasium," to which the reader is referred for a
greater variety of illustrations. But in all exercises without apparatus the principle of bodily erectitude must be
kept steadily in view or nothing will be gained. All
bending of the body must be at the hip-points, and in
lying, sitting, standing, walking, or running, playing, or

Fig 23.   Fig. 24.

ATTENTION.   MILITARY
                POSITION.

working, no position must be
maintained that bends the trunk
of the body or in any manner
restricts the play of the lungs,
or compresses the abdominal
viscera. The proper hint on this
subject is afforded in the familiar calisthenic illustrations (Figs.
23 and 24).

Keeping in mind the proper
military "attention" under all cir-
cumstances, the circular exercise
of the arms will be found an admirable one for bringing into
gentle and equal action the whole respiratory system
(Figs. 25 and 26).

This exercise is performed by extending the arms forward at right angles with the body, the palms of the
hands being turned toward each other, and then rotating
the arms alternately, then both together on the shoulder
joint. Count one at each rotation, and turn the hands,
during the movement, as far as possible both ways, so as
to secure the rolling motion of arms and joints. After

the movement has been performed half-a-dozen times in one direction, reverse it, and make as many movements

Figs. 25 and 26.—EXERCISE FOR THE WHOLE RESPIRATORY SYSTEM.

in the opposite direction; keep the palm of the hand down whenever the arm is raised.

The elbow whirl (fig. 27) may be performed as a variation of the above, and for very feeble persons, especially those troubled with shortness of breath, it is a good preparatory exercise. Place the elbows on the hips, and then swing the forearms in a circle.

The "circular" and "whirl" motions may be performed with increased effect while walking up hill or on an uneven surface.

The "lateral body swing" (fig. 28) is also an admirable preparatory exercise, and may vary the elbow whirl. This movement consists in bending the body from side to side, the arms being extended. It should be

ELBOW WHIRL.

performed very slowly at first, counting in a prolonged monotone to correspond with the bodily motions.

Fig. 28.

LATERAL MOVEMENT.

For those whose chests are contracted, who are round or stoopshouldered, or who are predisposed to consumption, the "chest extension" exercise is especially to be recommended (figs. 29, 30, and 31).

These exercises comprehend several movements of the arms, all of which are intended to stretch the muscles and ligaments more especially of the upper part of the chest. Hold the arms at right angles with the body, and then throw the arms and hands backward and forward with considerable force, counting at each backward motion. Then from the same commencing position, vary

Fig. 29.   Fig. 30.   Fig. 31.

CHEST EXTENSION EXERCISES.

the exercise by striking the elbows together behind (fig. 31).

For the benefit of those who have the ordinary calisthenic apparatus, the following familiar illustrations are given:

The Indian club exercise is calculated to develop powerfully the muscles of the arms and chest. Figs. 32, 33, 34, and 35 show the principal positions so far as club exercises especially affect the respiratory system.

Fig. 32.　　　Fig. 33.　　　Fig. 34.　　　Fig. 35.

INDIAN CLUB EXERCISES.

Weights and dumb-bells may be employed to intensify the effect of any of the exercises which are usually performed without apparatus; and in a variety of such other ways as any one, understanding the object in view, can readily extemporize. Figs. 36 and 37 are examples.

Backboards and bands, which require no special explanation, help make a variety of useful apparatus. Figs. 38 and

39 represent some of the usual methods of exercising with them.

Fig. 36.

Fig. 37.

EXERCISES WITH WEIGHTS.

The impediments of speech termed *lisping* and *stammering*, can generally be remedied without difficulty by a persevering course of vocal training, and reasonable attention to hygienic conditions. The fact that those who lisp and stammer in speaking, usually articulate well enough in singing, suggests the proper remedial plan. They should aim to get entire mental control of the vocal apparatus by enunciating all of the elementary sounds of the language very slowly,

Fig. 38.

Fig. 39.

EXERCISES WITH BACKBOARDS.

deliberately, and distinctly, until the habit of convulsive action of the affected muscles is overcome. The stammerer should always speak with an expiring breath, and with the mouth well opened; a cure can generally be accomplished in a few months, sometimes in a few weeks. Indeed, a proper and persevering course of vocal gymnastics will almost certainly remedy the worst kind of stammering.

The first thing for the stammerer to do is to get complete control of his breathing apparatus. This can be done by means of the exercises mentioned in the succeeding chapter, especially those recommended by Professor Zachos, combined with the practice of slow, deep, full, and prolonged respirations. After this is accomplished, exercises on the vowel sounds, as explained hereafter, will be in order, constituting what M. Chevril, of France, who has acquired a reputation for the successful treatment of vocal impediments, terms the "gymnastics of articular phonation." When these vowel sounds are so thoroughly mastered that they can be distinctly enunciated forward and backward (thirty-two sounds) with a single expiration; and without any appreciable tendency to spasmodic action, the consonant sounds should be practiced on until all of them can be enunciated without the least inclination to stammer. Lastly, all of the elementary sounds of our language (forty-four), as explained in the ensuing chapter, should be practiced on until every sound is made without difficulty. Says M. Chevril: "The whole plan consists in gymnastically educating the organs of speech, the excellent results being due not so much to actual muscular work as to the precision with which the practice is carried out. The success depends on an effort of the will on the part of the patient to reproduce with the utmost precision a particular sound. The will of the teacher must take the place of the patient's will, as the latter is unable to regulate the movements dictated by it."

The principle above indicated may be readily comprehended when it is considered that hiccough, which is a spasmodic action of some of the respiratory muscles, can always be arrested instantly by a strong effort of the will properly directed. It is only necessary to fix the attention on some subject or object intensely; for example, the patient may determine to speak the word hiccough, *during* the next "attack," or paroxysm, and then watch intently for the first indication of it. If his attention is intense enough he will not hiccough again.

CHAPTER V.

In all exercises having in view the improvement of the vocal apparatus, the first consideration as already stated, is a correct bodily position. It should be easy, unconstrained, and in all respects natural, allowing the freest play to every muscle concerned in respiration as well as vocalization. Figs. 40, 41, 42, and 43 represent some of the normal positions in public speaking.

PRESERVATION OF THE VOICE.

The rules for ensuring the durability and best working condition of the voice are few, simple, and mainly negative.

1. Be temperate in all things—and this means, avoid

Fig. 40.

DECLAMATION.

Fig. 41.

ARGUMENT.

(41)

gluttony and dissipation, and be moderate in all sensuous indulgences.

2. Do not make violent vocal efforts soon after a full meal; nor exert the voice at its highest pitch long at a

Fig. 42.

EXHORTATION.

Fig. 43.

APPEAL.

time. Never use the voice except very moderately when affected with hoarseness.

3. Butter, nuts, old cheese, sugar, candies, salted meats, acid liquors, ice-cream, very cold drinks, and very hot drinks, are especially injurious to the voice.

CONTROLLING THE RESPIRATION.

Among the essentials of good reading or speaking is a perfect command of the breath, so that all of the expired air can be used to the utmost advantage in vocalization. To acquire this condition :

1. Read or declaim in a *loud* whisper. This exercise is very fatiguing at first, and should be practiced but a few minutes at a time, until habit renders it easy.

2. Read or declaim in a low, strong key, passages which

require a firm and dignified enunciation, gradually proceeding to more spirited, and finally to the most impassioned sentences.

3. The following respiratory exercises, recommended by Prof. Zachos, are admirable for enabling the speaker to express the deeper emotions:

Full Breathing.—Stand in an erect position, with the arms akimbo, the hands resting on the hips; slowly draw in the breath until the chest is fully expanded; emit it with the utmost slowness.

Audible Breathing.—Draw in the breath as in full breathing, and expire it audibly, as in the prolonged sound of the letter k.

Forcible Breathing.—Fill the lungs, and then let out the breath suddenly and forcibly, in the manner of an abrupt and whispered cough.

Sighing.—Fill suddenly the lungs with a full breath, and emit as quickly as possible.

Gasping.—With a convulsive effort inflate the lungs; then send forth the breath more gently.

Panting.—Breath quickly and violently, making the emission of breath loud and forcible.

MANAGEMENT OF THE VOICE.

The proper management of the voice comprises due attention to tones, accent, emphasis, pronunciation, articulation, and pauses. The following rules should be observed:

1. Commence speaking a little *under* the ordinary pitch of voice.

2. The principal part of a discourse should be delivered in the ordinary pitch of voice; the exordium should be very deliberate and below the ordinary pitch, and the

peroration more impassioned and above the ordinary pitch.

THE REGULATION OF TONES.

Nothing is more awkward in public speaking than a misadaptation of tones to the occasion. They may be classified as follows:

1. The whisper, intended to be audible only to the nearest person.

2. The murmur, or low tone, adapted to close conversation.

3. The ordinary pitch, suited to general conversation.

4. The high or elevated pitch, adapted only to earnest argument or powerful appeals.

5. The extreme or highest pitch, appropriate only in the expression of violent passions.

ENUNCIATION.

Guard against the common fault of reading or speaking with the mouth insufficiently opened, or the teeth nearly closed. If this habit has been acquired, overcome it as speedily as possible. This may be done by reciting occasionally with a gag placed between the teeth; it may be made of card-board or a thin piece of wood. Commence with a gag half an inch wide, and gradually increase it to an inch and a half.

Be careful to articulate every syllable of every word. The general fault of readers, speakers, and especially singers, is in failing to articulate unaccented syllables. The rule of pronunciation is to regard every syllable as equally important, giving each its proper sound, and never slurring nor blending them together.

DEPORTMENT.

Under this head a few words on the countenance, manner, and gesture may be proper.

Nothing tends more to secure the sympathies of the audience than a quiet, self-possessed deportment. Never come before an audience, nor approach the speaker's desk in a hurried, bustling manner. Be deliberate and natural. *Be right, then act yourself.* Look over the audience, but do not stare *at* it. Avoid all awkward and uncouth expressions of countenance, as pouting, stretching, or twisting the lips; do not bite, smack, nor lick the lips; in enunciating emphatic words or sentences, do not pull down the corners of the mouth and expose the teeth as in grinning; the mouth should be used much more than the lips in forcible speaking.

In all proper gesticulation the movements of the body correspond with and express, in the language of signs, the thoughts and feelings of the speaker. This is done normally by young children, and by all persons who have not been perverted by miseducation. The tendency of the teachings of most of our schools is to exaggeration, by which the student acquires an artificial and affected mannerism. It is propriety, not quantity, of gesture that should be studied. The person who forgets himself in his subject seldom errs in gesticulation, while the person who puts himself before his subject always does. The question for the speaker, who would become proficient in gesture, to ask himself, is not, "What do the hearers think of *me?*" but "How do I present the subject?" If the speaker successfully communicates his thoughts and feelings to others, he will most certainly do himself justice in manner.

In standing, rest alternately on each foot, and prin-

cipally on the heel, changing position frequently. Keep
the feet always flat on the floor, avoiding all tendency to
rest on the toes or on one edge of either foot. In walking
the stage, turn by placing one foot behind the other, thus
at all times inclining to face the audience; never make
the awkward blunder of turning one foot around the
other in front, thus bringing the back to the audience.
The grace of oratorical action consists in the freedom and
simplicity of those gestures which illustrate the subject.

On this subject the reader who aims at excellence will
do well to read Pittenger's " Oratory, Sacred and Secular,"
which gives a history of some of the leading orators,
preachers, and lecturers of the present day, and of the
preceding century.

CHAPTER VI.

THOSE who would excel as speakers, readers, or singers, should be able to enunciate, distinctly and rapidly, all of the primary or elementary sounds which are represented by written language. The twenty-six letters of the English alphabet represent forty-four distinct sounds, as explained in the following table:

ANALYSIS OF THE ELEMENTARY SOUNDS.

There are forty-four sounds of the English language, represented by the twenty-six letters of the alphabet and their combinations, as in the following table:

1. a, long, as in ale, pale, national, plaintiff, amen.
2. a, grave, or Italian, as in ah, far, papa, mamma.
3. a, broad, or German, as in all, draw, daughter, fraught.
4. a, short, as in at, hat, attack, malefactor.
5. b, name sound, as in be, bite, bright, tub, hubbub .
6. c, sound of s, as in cent, city, cornice, precipice.
7. c, sound of k, as in cap, come, occult, ecliptic.
8. c, sound of z, as in suffice, discern, sacrifice.
9. c, sound of sh, as in ocean, Phocion, Cappadocia.
10. d, name sound, as in ride, did, daddy, double-headed.
11. d, sound of t, as in faced, watched, dipped, escaped.
12. e, long, as in eel, peel, creed, reveal, precede.
13. e, short, as in ell, expel, ever-extended.
14. f, name sound, as in if, rife, fife, faithful, tariff.
15. f, sound of v, as in of, hereof, whereof, thereof.

(47)

16. g, soft or name sound, as in gem, ginseng, logical.
17. { g, hard, as in go, give, gig, Brobdignag.
18. g, sound of gh, as in rouge, protege, mirage.
19. h, name sound, as in hale, high, Hannah.
20. } i, long, as in isle, lilac, oblige, iodine.
21. { i, short, as in in, pin, king, distinctive.
22. l, name sound, as in lo, lily, dalliance, lullaby.
23. m, name sound, as in map, mummy, amalgamate.
24. { n, name sound, as in nine, ninny, nobleman, manikin.
25. { n, sound of ng, as in bank, ingot, congress, angular.
26. o, long, as in old, osier, trophy, sofa, atrocious.
27. { o, close, as in ooze, douceur, accoutre, troubadour.
28. o, short, as in on, combat, obelisk, holyday.
29. p, name sound, as in pill, pippin, panter, platter.
30. { r, smooth, as in war, afar, tartar, murderer.
31. { r, trilled, as in rough, railroad, recreation.
32. u, long, as in mute, astute, educate, judicature.
33. { u, short, as in up, mum, ultra, numbskull.
34. u, full, as in pull, cruel, Prussian, Brutus.
35. w, name sound, as in woo, bewail, wigwam, wormwood.
36. } x, name sound, as in axe, coxcomb, luxury, example.
37. { x, sound of gz, as in exist, exhibit, exuberant.
38. y, name sound, as in ye, yoke, yewyaw, yesterday.
39. ch, name sound, as in charm, church, chickering, Chimborazo.
40. { th, aspirate, as in thin, think, thankless, prothonotary.
41. { th, vocal, as in than, that, beneath, withhold, wherewithal.
42. wh, name sound, as in what, wherefore, whirligig, whimpering.
43. oi or oy, diphthongs, or digraphs, as in oil, boy, recoil, employ.
44. ou or ow, diphthongs, or digraphs, as in our, bow, gouty, trowel.

The student should master all of these sounds, and practice on them until he can repeat them with facility backward or forward; after which he may, with advantage, exercise on the different sounds or groups of sounds, with the view of developing the power of particular portions of the vocal and respiratory apparatus.

ANALYSIS OF THE SOUNDS OF LETTERS.

In order to ascertain the exact sound represented by any letter, character, or combination of letters, the student has only to analyze a word in which it occurs. The process is a very simple one, yet many teachers have never learned it.

Ask the scholar in the primary school, "How many sounds has b?" and he may answer promptly, "B has but one sound, as in bite." Very well; then ask him, "What *is* that sound of b, as in bite?" and he may not be able to tell you.

To ascertain what the sound of b is, and to be able to make it, pure and simple, he has only to analyze, vocally, any word or syllable containing the letter. It is more convenient for new beginners to take a word commencing with the letter, "as in bite." Let him spell and pronounce all the letters in the usual manner—b-i-t-e, bite. Then spell and pronounce all except the last letter, e—b-i-t, bit. The i being long, as in isle, the pronunciation of bite is precisely the same without the terminal e as with it; hence the scholar discovers that e is silent in that word. Next let him spell and pronounce the word, omitting the last two letters, t and e—b-i, bi. He now learns that i has its long sound in that word; if it were short it would be sounded like i in hit. Lastly let him sound the word, omitting the last three letters. He will then enunciate the one sound of b, as in bite; and a little attention to the vocal organs will show him precisely how the sound of b is made.

The process of analysis is now completed; and by observing the position and action of the lips, he learns why the letter b belongs to the category of *labial* or lip sounds, its pronunciation, as well as that of m and p, requiring a closure of the lips.

By the application of this key the student can readily ascertain the sound of any letter or character.

Another similar and still more simple method is, to

3

select a word beginning with the letter or character the
sound of which is to be ascertained; commence the pronunciation of the word, but stop the effort instantly with
the first sound which the ear recognizes; this will be the
pure sound by itself, whether vocal or aspirate.

Thus, if the student begin to pronounce the names,
Cicero and Cato, and the words, this and thin, and inter-
rupts the effort with the first appreciable noise, he will
learn that c in Cicero has the hissing sound of s, and c in
Cato the hard sound of k; while th in the word this,
has a compound vocal sound, and th in thin, a compound
aspirate or breath sound.

EXERCISES ON THE VOWEL SOUNDS.

There are sixteen vowel sounds in our language, in-
cluding the diphthongs; they are found in the order of our
alphabet in the following words: *ale, ah, all, at, eel, ell,
isle, ill, old, ooze, on, use, up, full, oil, how.* The enunciation of these vowel sounds, distinct from that of the consonant sounds, in reading, speaking, and singing, is one of
the best exercises for acquiring flexibility of the articulating muscles, and elasticity of the vocal cords; also for
bringing into vigorous co-operative action those respiratory muscles which are most immediately concerned in
the production of the lower tones of voice. They should
be pronounced forward and backward until they can be
repeated several times with a single respiration, thus:

ale, ah, all, at, eel, ell, isle, ill, old, ooze, on, use, up-
full oil, how, a, a, a, a, e, e, i, i, o, o, o, u, u, w, oi, ow.

Reversely,

ow, oi, u, u, u, o, o, o, i, i, e, e, a, a, a, a, how, oil, full,
up, use, on, ooze, old, ill, isle, ell, eel, at, all, ah, ale.

This exercise may be advantageously varied by employing only the short vowel sounds in the same manner. at, ell, ill, on, up—up, on, ill, ell, at, a, e, i, o, u—u, o, i, e, a.

Reading by the vowel sounds alone, is an exceedingly useful exercise for the articulating muscles, and may serve to " vary the entertainment." No better example for practice can be found than Hamlet's advice to the players.

Speak the speech, I pray you, as *I* pronounced it to you; *trippingly*
e   e e ,i a u,a i o ou   i o u; i i i
on the tongue. But if you *mouth* it, as *many* of our players do, I had
o e   u. u i u ou i,a a i o ou a e o,i a
as lief the town-*crier* had spoke my lines. And do not saw the *air* too
a e e ou i e a o i i . a o o a e a o
much with your *hand;* but use all *gently;* for in the very *torrent*,
u, i u a ; u u a e i; o i e e i o e ,
tempest, and, as I may say, WHIRLWIND of your passion, you must
e e,,a ,a i a a, i i o u a u, u u
acquire and beget a *temperance* that may give it *smoothness*. Oh! it
a i a e e a e a a a i i o e. o i
offends me to the *soul* to hear a *robustious periwig*-pated fellow, tear a
o e   e o e o o e a o u i u e i i a e e o, a a
passion to *tatters*, to very *rags*, to split the ears of the *groundlings*.
a u o a e , o o i a , o i ee o e o . i .

EXERCISES ON THE CONSONANT SOUNDS.

There are seventeen *vocal* and eleven *aspirate* sounds in the English language; consonants are also distinguished into *simple*, of which there are thirteen, and *compound*, of which there are fifteen.

CONSONANTS. { *Vocal.*—b, as in bite; c, as in discern; d, as in dome; f, as in thereof; g, as in gem; g, as in go; g, as in menagerie; l, as in line; m, as in mamma; n, as in not; n, as in clank; r, as in jar; r, as in bright; w, as in wist; x, as in excite; y, as in youth; th, as in thee.

CONSONANTS.

Aspirate.—c, as in cent; c, as in cap; c, as in gracious; d, as in embraced; f, as in fit; h, as in hand; p, as in pop; x, as in extant; ch, as in chance; th, as in thin; wh, as in whine.

Simple.—b, as in bib; c, as in circle; c, as in Connecticut; d, as in day; d, as in tripp'd; f, as in foe; g, as in give; h, as in hope; l, as in live; m, as in man; n, as in ten; p, as in poppy; r, as in more.

Compound.—c, sound of z, as in suffice; c, sound of sh, as in judicial; f, sound of v, as in hereof; g, soft, as in ginger; g, sound of zh, as in tongue; n, sound of ng, as in Frank; r, rough or trilled, as in crash; w, name sound, as in wool; x, sound of ks, as in excel; x, sound of gz, as in example; y, name sound, as in yarn; ch, sound of tch, as in much; th, soft, or aspirate, as in theme; th, vocal, as in thou; wh, name sound, as in when.

Every consonant sound should be distinctly recognized and enunciated, until the whole list of twenty-eight can be repeated forward and backward with a single respiration. Exercises on the consonant sounds are calculated to promote rapidity and accuracy in the action of the tongue, lips, and mouth.

The following words represent the consonant sounds in the order heretofore mentioned : bob, cent, come, suffice, ocean, ride, dipped, rife, of, gem, go, mirage, hale, lo, man, nine, bank, pin, war, rough, wo, axe, exist, yoke, charm, thin, than, what.

By analyzing these words in the manner already explained, the sound represented by each letter or combination of letters will be readily ascertained.

EXERCISES IN EMPHASIS.

Stress.—The *first* three, and the *last* two verses, or volumes; not the *three* first and the *two* last; there can be only *one first* thing.

Quantity.—Roll on, thou dark and deep blue ocean— roll! Ten thousand fleets sweep over thee in vain. Hail! —universal Lord.

Expulsive Stress.—Aim at nothing higher until you can read and speak deliberately, clearly, distinctly, and with the appropriate emphasis.

Stress and Higher Pitch.—O man, tyrannic lord! how long—how long, shall prostrate nature groan beneath your rage!

Prolongation and Monotone.—I appeal to you—O ye hills and groves of Alba, and your demolished altars! I call you to witness!—and thou—O holy Jupiter!

Rhetorical Pause.—Will all great Neptune's ocean wash this blood—clean—from my hands? No, these, my hands, will rather the multitudinous sea incarnadine, making the green—one red.

Change of the Seat of Accent.—Temperance and virtue raise men above themselves to angels; intemperance and vice sink them below themselves to the level of brutes.

SHOUTING.

Charge! Chester! charge! on Stanley, on;
Liberty, freedom—tyranny is dead;
Run hence; proclaim it in the streets—
The combat deepens! ON, *ye brave!*

EXAMPLES OF INTONATIONS.

Rising.—Are you desirous of becoming a good reader, speaker, and singer? Then learn and practice the principles herein taught and demonstrated.

Falling.—A mind properly disciplined to submit to a small present evil, to obtain a greater distant good, will often reap victory from defeat and honor from repulse.

Rising and Falling.—To whom the goblin, full of wrath, replied: Art thou traitor angel? Art thou he who first broke peace in heaven, and faith till then unbroken? Back to the punishment—false fugitive!

The man who is in the daily use of ardent spirits, if he does not become a drunkard, is in danger of losing his health and character.

EXAMPLES OF WAVES OR CIRCUMFLEXES.

Rising.—The love of approbation—produces excellent effects on men of sense; a strong desire for praise in weak minds conduces to little else than vanity.

Falling.—It is not prudent to trust your secrets to a man who can not keep his own. If you had made that affirmation, I might perhaps have believed it.

Combination.—Mere hirelings and time-servers—are always opposed to improvements and originality: so are tyrants—to liberty and republicanism.

CADENCE.

Ye nymphs of Solyma, begin the song;
To heavenly themes sublimer strains belong.

Such honors Ilion to her lover paid,
And peaceful slept the mighty Hector's shade.

EXAMPLES OF DYNAMICS.

Loud.—With mighty crash the noise astounds; amid Carnarvon's mountains rages loud, the repercussive roar; and Tliule bellows through her utmost isles.

Rough.—The tempest growls; the unconquerable lightning struggles through, ragged and fierce, and—raging, strikes the aggravating rocks.

SOFT.

Soft roll your incense, herbs, and fruits, and flowers
Ye softer floods, that lead the humid maze
Along the vale.   Breathe your still song
Into the reaper's heart.

SMOOTH.

Perfumes as of Eden flowed sweetly along,
And a voice as of angels enchantingly sung.

And the smooth stream in smoother numbers flowed.

Harsh.—On a sudden, open fly with impetuous recoil and jarring sound the infernal doors, and on their groaning hinges grate harsh thunder.

Forcible.—Now storming fury rose, and clamor, such as heard in heaven, till now, was never; arms on armor clashing, brayed horrible discord.

Harmonious.—As earth asleep, unconscious lies; effuse your mildest beams, ye constellations, while your angels strike, amid the spangled sky, the silver lyre.

Strong.—Him the Almighty power hurled headlong, flaming from the ethereal skies, with hideous ruin and combustion down to bottomless perdition.

CHAPTER VII.

THE student who aims at excellence in speaking or writing should carefully study, and become familiar with, the spirit of the masters of elocution and composition. He will profit more in studying well, practicing thoroughly, on a single production from one of their pens, than by memorizing and declaiming a hundred indifferent compositions by second-rate authors. Booth, Jefferson, Salvini, and Cushman, by mastering the characters of Hamlet, Rip Van Winkle, Othello, and Meg Merrilies, can have a profitable field of action for a life-time in playing those characters alone. One thing well done, in elocution as in other vocations, prepares the way for doing other things well, and leads the way to honor and prosperity.

In the following selections the masters of language and of oratory are represented, and their productions may not be excelled for ages. The selections are arranged with the view to public declamation as well as private exercise.

TO RANGE.

Strike home, strong-hearted man! down to the root
Of old oppression sink the Saxon steel.
Thy work is to hew down. In God's name, then,
Put nerve into thy task. Let other men

(56)

Plant, as they may, that better tree, whose fruit,
The wounded bosom of the church shall heal,
Be thou the image-breaker. Let thy blows
Fall heavily as the Suabian's iron hand,
On crown or crosier, which shall interpose
Between thee and the weal of Father-land.
Leave creeds to closet idlers. First of all,
Shake thou all German dream-land with the fall
Of that accursed tree, whose evil trunk
Was spared of old by Erfart's stalwart monk.
Fight not with ghosts and shadows. Let us hear
The snap of chain-links. Let our gladdened ear
Catch the pale prisoner's welcome, as the light
Follows thy axe-stroke, through his cell of night.
Be faithful to both worlds ; nor think to feed
Earth's starving millions with the husks of creed.
Servant of Him whose mission high and holy
Was to the wronged, the sorrowing, and the lowly,
Thrust not His Eden promise from our sphere,
Distant and dim beyond the blue sky's span;
Like him of Patmos, see it, now and here,—
The New Jerusalem comes to man!
Be warned by Luther's error. Nor like him,
When the routed Tuton dashes from his limb
The rusted chain of ages, help to bind
His hands, for whom thou claim'st the freedom of the
  mind!

GLORY.

1. The crumbling tombstone and the gorgeous mauso-
le'um, the sculptured marble, and the venerable cathe-
dral, all bear witness to the instinctive desire within us
to be remembered by coming generations. But how
short-lived is the immortality which the works of our
hands can confer! The noblest monuments of art that
the world has ever seen are covered with the soil of
twenty centuries. The works of the age of Pericles lie

3*

at the foot of the Acropolis in indiscriminate ruin. The plow-share turns up the marble which the hand of Phidias had chiseled into beauty, and the Mussulman has folded his flock beneath the falling columns of the temple of Minerva.

2. But even the works of our hands too frequently survive the memory of those who have created them. And were it otherwise, could we thus carry down to distant ages the recollection of our existence, it were surely childish to waste the energies of an immortal spirit in the effort to make it known to other times, that a being whose name was written with certain letters of the alphabet, once lived, and flourished, and died. Neither sculptured marble, nor stately column, can reveal to other ages the lineaments of the spirit; and these alone can embalm our memory in the hearts of a grateful prosperity.

3. As the stranger stands beneath the dome of St. Paul's, or treads, with religious awe, the silent aisles of Westminster Abbey, the sentiment, which is breathed from every object around him, is, the utter emptiness of sublunary glory. The fine arts, obedient to private affection or public gratitude, have here embodied, in every form, the finest conceptions of which their age was capable. Each one of these monuments has been watered by the tears of the widow, the orphan, or the patriot.

4. But generations have passed away, and mourners and mourned have sunk together into forgetfulness. The aged crone, or the smooth-tongued beadle, as now he hurries you through ailes and chapel, utters, with measured cadence and unmeaning tone, for the thousandth time, the name and lineage of the once honored dead; and then gladly dismisses you, to repeat again his well-conned lesson to another group of idle passers-by.

5. Such, in its most august form, is all the immortality that matter can confer. It is by what we ourselves have done, and not by what others have done for us, that we shall be remembered by after ages. It is by thought that has aroused my intellect from its slumbers, which has "given lustre to virtue, and dignity to truth," or by those examples which have inflamed my soul with the love of goodness, and not by means of sculptured marble, that I hold communion with Shakespeare and Milton, with Johnson and Burke, with Howard and Wilberforce.

DR. WAYLAND.

CATO'S SOLILOQUY.

1 It must be so—Plato, thou reasonest well!
Else, whence this pleasing hope, this fond desire,
This longing after immortality?
Or whence this secret dread, and inward horror,
Of falling into naught? Why shrinks the soul
Back on herself, and startles at destruction?
'Tis the divinity that stirs within us;
'Tis Heaven itself that points out a hereafter,
And intimates eternity to man.

2 Eternity!—though pleasing, dreadful thought!
Through what variety of untried being,
Through what new scenes and changes must we pass!
The wide, the unbounded prospect lies before me;
But shadows, clouds, and darkness rest upon it.
Here will I hold. If there's a Power above us,—
And that there is, all Nature cries aloud
Through all her works,—He must delight in virtue;
And that which He delights in must be happy.
But when? or where? This world was made for Cæsar.
I'm weary of conjectures,—this must end them.
                    [Laying his hand on his sword.

3 Thus am I doubly armed. My death and life,
My bane and antidote, are both before me.

This in a moment brings me to my end;
But this informs me I shall never die.
The soul, secure in her existence, smiles
At the drawn dagger, and defies its point.
The stars shall fade away, the sun himself
Grow dim with age, and Nature sink in years;
But thou shalt flourish in immortal youth,
Unhurt amid the war of elements,
The wreck of matter, and the crush of worlds.

ADDISON.

OUR HONORED DEAD.

1. How bright are the honors which await those who
with sacred fortitude and pātriŏt'ic patience have endured
all things that they might save their native land from
division and from the power of corruption! 'The honored dead! They that die for a good cause are redeemed
from death. Their names are gắthered and garnered.
Their memory is precious. Each place grows proud for
them who were born there.

2. There is to be, ere lŏng, in ĕvẻry village and in
every neighborhood, a glowing pride in its martyred
heroes. Tablets shall preserve their names. Pious love
shall renew their inscriptions as time and the unfeeling
elements decay them. And the nătional festivals shall
give multitudes of precious names to the ŏrator's lips.
Children shall grow up under mōre sacred inspirations,
whose elder brothers, dying nobly for their country, left
a name that honored and inspired all who bore it. Orphan children shall find thousands of fathers and mothers
to love and help those whom dying heroes left as a legacy
to the gratitude of the public.

3. Oh, tell me not that they are dead—that generous
hŏst, that airy army of invisible heroes! They hover as
a cloud of witnẻssẻs above this nation. Are they dead

that yĕt speak louder than we can speak, and a mōre universal language? Are they dead that yet act? Are they
dead that yet move upon society, and inspire the people
with nobler motives and more heroic pātriŏtĭsm?

4. Ye that mōurn, let gladnèss mingle with your tears.
He *was* your son; but now he *is* the nation's. He made
your household bright: now his example inspires a thousand households. Dear to his brothers and sisters, he is
now brother to ĕvèry generous youth in the land. Before, he was nărrowed, appropriated, shut up to you.
Now he is augmented, set free, and given to all. He has
died from the fămily, that he might live to the nation.
Not one name shall be forgotten or neglected; and it
shall by-and-by be confessed, as of an āncient hērō, that
he did more for his country by his death than by his
whōle life.

5. Nēither are they less honored who shall bear through
life the marks of wounds and sufferings. Neither ĕp'au-
lĕtte nor badge is so honorable as wounds received in a
good cause. Many a man shall envy him who hencefōrth
limps. So strānge is the transforming power of pātriŏtic
ardor, that men shall almost covet disfigurement. Crowds
will give way to hobbling cripples, and uncover in the
presence of feeblenèss and helplessness. And buoyant
children shall pause in their noisy games, and with lov-
ing reverence honor them whose hands can work no
more, and whose feet are no longer able to march except
upon that journey which brings good men to honor and
immortality.

6. O mother of lŏst children! set not in darknèss nor
sorrow whom a nation honors. O mōurners of the early
dead! they shall live again, and live forever. Your sór-
rows are our gladness. The nation lives, because you

gave it men that loved it better than their own lives. And when a few mŏre days shall have cleared the pĕrils from around the nation's brow, and she shall sit in unsullied garments of liberty, with justice upon her fŏrehĕad, love in her eyes, and truth npon her lips, she shall not forget those whose blood gave vital cŭrrents to her heart, and whose life, given to her, shall live with her life till time shall be no more.

7. Every mountain and hill shall have its treasured name, every river shall keep some solemn title, every valley and every lake shall cherish its honored register; and till the mountains are wŏrn out, and the rivers forget to flow, till the clouds are weary of replenishing springs, and the springs forget to gush, and the rills to ѕing, shall their names be kept fresh with reverent honŏrs, which are inscribed upon the book of National Remembrance!

H. W. BEECHER.

DARKNESS.

1. I had a dream, which was not all a dream.
The bright sun was extinguished, and the stars
Did wander, darkling, in the eternal space,
Raylĕss and pathless, and the icy earth
Swung blind and blackening in the moonless air.
Morn came, and went—and came, and brought no day,
And men forgot their passions, in the dread
Of this their desolation; and all hearts
Were chilled into a selfish prayer for light.
And they did live by watch-fires; and the thrones,
The palaces of crownéd kings, the huts,
The habitations of all things which dwell,
Were burnt for bĕacons: cities were consumed,
And men were gathered round their blazing homes,
To look once mŏre into each other's face.
Happy were those who dwelt within the eye
Of the volcanoes and their mountain torch.

2. A fearful hope was all the world contained:
　Forests were set on fire; but hour by hour,
　They fell and faded; and the crackling trunks
　Extinguished with a crash—and all was black.
　The brows of men, by their despairing light,
　Wore an unearthly aspect, as, by fits,
　The flashes fell upon them. Some lay down,
　And hid their eyes, and wept; and some did rest
　Their chins upon their clenchèd hands, and smiled;
　And others hurried to and fro, and fed
　Their funeral piles with fuel, and looked up,
　With mad disquietude, on the dull sky,
　The pall of a past world ; and then again
　With curses, cast them down upon the dust,
　And gnashed their teeth, and howled. The wild birds
　　shrieked,
　And, terrified, did flutter on the ground,
　And flap their useless wings: the wildest brutes
　Came tame and tremulous; and vipers crawled
　And twined themselves among the multitude,
　Hissing, but stingless—they were slain for food.

3. And War, which for a moment was no more,
　Did glut himself again:—a meal was bought
　With blood, and each sat sullenly apart,
　Gorging himself in gloom; no love was left;
　All earth was but one thought—and that was death,
　Immediate and inglorious; and the pang
　Of famine fed upon all entrails. Men
　Died; and their bones were tombless as their flesh.
　The meager by the meager were devoured.
　Even dogs assailed their masters,—all save one,
　And he was faithful to a corpse, and kept
　The birds, and beasts, and famished men at bay,
　Till hunger clung them or the drooping dead
　Lured their lank jaws: himself sought out no food,
　But with a piteous and perpetual moan,
　And a quick, desolate cry, licking the hand
　Which answered not with a caress—he died.

4. The crowd was famished by degrees. But two
  Of an enormous city did survive,
  And they were enemies. They met beside
  The dying embers of an altar-place,
  Where had been heaped a mass of holy things
  For an unholy usage. They raked up,
  And, shivering, scraped with their cold skeleton hands,
  The feeble ashes, and their feeble breath
  Blew for a little life, and made a flame,
  Which was a mockery. Then they lifted
  Their eyes as it grew lighter, and beheld
  Each other's aspects—saw, and shrieked, and died;
  Even of their mutual hideousness they died,
  Unknowing who he was upon whose brow
  Famine had written Fiend.

5.   The world was void:
  The populous and the powerful was a lump,—
  Seasonless, herbless, treeless, manless, lifeless;
  A lump of death, a chaos of hard clay.
  The rivers, lakes, and ocean all stood still,
  And nothing stirred within their silent depths.
  Ships, sailorless, lay rotting on the sea,
  And their masts fell down piecemeal: as they dropped
  They slept on the abyss, without a surge,—
  The waves were dead ; the tides were in their grave;
  The moon, their mistress, had expired before;
  The winds were withered in the stagnant air,
  And the clouds perished: Darkness had no need
  Of aid from them—she was the universe.

LORD BYRON.

A CURTAIN LECTURE OF MRS. CAUDLE.

Bah! that's the third umbrella gone since Christmas.
What were you to do? Why, let him go home in the
rain, to be sure. I'm very certain there was nothing
about him that could spoil.—Take cold, indeed! He
doesn't look like one of the sort to take cold. Besides he'd

have better taken cold than taken our umbrella.—Do you hear the rain, Mr. Caudle? I say, do you hear the rain? And, as I'm alive, if it isn't St. Swithin's day! Do you hear it against the windows? Nonsense! you don't im_pose upon me; you can't be asleep with such a shower as that! Do you hear it, I say? Oh! you DO hear it! Well, that's a pretty flood, I think, to last for six weeks; and no stirring all the time out of the house.

2. Pooh! don't think me a fool, Mr. Caudle; don't insult me; *he* return the umbrella! Anybody would think you were born yĕsterday. As if anybody ever did return an umbrella! There: do you hear it? Worse and worse. Cats and dŏgs, and for six weeks: always six weeks; and no umbrella!—I should like to know how the children are to go to school to-mŏrrow! They shan't go through such weather; I am determined. No; they shall stop at home and never learn any thing (the blessèd creatures!) sooner than go and gĕt wet! And when they grow up, I wonder who they'll have to thank for knowing nothing: who, indeed, but their father. People who can't feel for their own children ought never to be fathers.

3. But I know why you lent the umbrella: oh! yes, I know vĕry well. I was going out to tea at dear mother's to-mŏrrow: you knew that, and you did it on purpose. Don't tell me; you hate to have me go there, and take every mean advantage to hinder me. But don't you think it, Mr. Caudle; no, sir: if it comes down in bucket-fulls, I'll go all the mōre. No; and I wōn't have a cab! Where do you think the money's to come from? You've got nice high notions at that club of yours! A cab, indeed! Cŏst me sixteen pence, at least. Sixteen pence! two-and-eight pence; for there's back again. Cabs, indeed! I should like to know who's to pay for 'em; for

I'm sure you can't, if you go on as you do, throwing away your property, and beggaring your children, buying umbrellas!

4. Do you hear the rain, Mr. Caudle? I say, do you hear it? But I don't care—I'll go to mother's to-morrow —I will; and what's more, I'll walk every step of the way; and you know that will give me my death. Don't call me a foolish woman; it's you that's the foolish man. You know I can't wear clogs; and with no umbrella, the wet's sure to give me a cold: it always does; but what do you care for that? Nothing at all. I may be laid up, for what you care, as I dare say I shall; and a pretty doctor's bill there'll be. I hope there will. It will teach you to lend your umbrellas again. I shouldn't wonder if I caught my death: yĕs, and that's what you lent the umbrella for. Of cōurse!

5. Nice clothes I gĕt, too, traipsing through weather like this. My gown and bŏnnet will be spoiled quite. Needn't I wear 'em, then? Indeed, Mr. Caudle, I *shall* wear 'em. No, sir; I'm not going out a dowdy, to please you, or anybody else. Gracious knows! it isn't ŏf*ten* that I step over the threshold:—indeed, I might as well be a slave at once: better, I should say; but when I do go out, Mr. Caudle, I choose to go as a lady.

6. Oh! that rain—if it isn't enough to break in the windōws. Ugh! I look forward with dread for to-mŏrrōw! How am I to go to mother's, I'm sure I can't tell; but if I die, I'll do it.—No, sir; I wŏn't bŏrrōw an umbrella: no; and you shan't *buy* one. Mr. Caudle, if you bring home another umbrella, I'll throw it into the street. Ha! And it was ōnly last week I had a new nozzle put to that umbrella. I'm sure if I'd have known as much as I do now, it might have gōne without one. Paying for new

nozzles for other people to laugh at you! Oh! it's all very well for you; you can go to sleep. You've no thought of your poor patient wife, and your own dear children; you think of nothing but lending umbrellas! Men, indeed!—call themselves lords of the creation! pretty lords, when they can't even take care of an umbrella!

7. I know that walk to-morrow will be the death of me. But that's what you want: then you may go to your club, and do as you like; and then nicely my poor dear children will be used; but then, sir, then you'll be happy. Oh! don't tell me! I know you will: else you'd never have lent the umbrella!—You have to go on Thursday about that summons; and, of course, you can't go. No, indeed: you *don't* go without the umbrella. You may lose the debt, for what I care—it won't be so much as spoiling your clothes—better lose it: people deserve to lose debts who lend umbrellas!

8. And I should like to know how I'm to go to mother's without the umbrella. Oh! don't tell me that I said I *would* go; that's nothing to do with it,—nothing at all. She'll think I'm neglecting her; and the little money we're to have, we shan't have at all;—because we've no umbrella.—The children, too! (dear things!) they'll be sopping wet: for they shan't stay at home; they shan't lose their learning; it's all their father will leave them, I'm sure! But they *shall* go to school. Don't tell me they shouldn't (you are so aggravating, Caudle, you'd spoil the temper of an angel!); they *shall* go to school: mark that! and if they get their deaths of cold, it's not my fault; I DIDN'T LEND THE UMBRELLA.   JERROLD.

IMMORTALITY.

"Man, thou shalt never die!" Celestial voices
Hymn it unto our souls: according harps,

By ăngel fingers touched, when the mild stars
Of morning sang together, sound fŏrth still
The sŏng of our great immortality!
Thick-clustering orbs on this our fair domain,
The tall, dark mountains, and the deep-tŏned seas,
Join in this solemn, universal song.
O lis*t*en, ye our spirits! drink it in
From all the air! 'Tis in the gentle moonlight; -
'Tis flŏating 'mid day's setting glŏries; night,
Wrapped in her sable robe, with silent step
Comes to our bed, and breathes it in our ears.
Night and the dawn, bright day and thoughtful eve,
All time, all bounds, the limitlèss expanse,
As one vast mȳstic instrument, are touched
By an unseen, living hand, and conscious chords
Quiver with joy in this great jubilee:
The dying hear it; and, as sounds of earth
Grow dull and distant, wake their passing souls
To mingle in this heavenly harmony."

R. H. DANA.

ADVANTAGES OF ADVERSITY.

1. From the dark pŏrtals of the stär-chămber, and in the
stern text of the acts of uniformity, the Pilgrims received a commission, mŏre efficient than any that ever
bŏre the royal seal. Their banishment to Holland was
fortunate; the decline of their little company in the
stränge land was fortunate; the difficulties which they
experienced in gĕtting the royal consent to banish themselves to this wilderness were fortunate; all the tears and
heart-breakings of that memorable parting at Delfthaven
had the happiĕst influence on the rising destinies of New
England. All this purified the ranks of the settlers.
These rough touches of fortune brushed ŏff the light, uncertain, selfish spirits. They made it a grave, solemn,
self-denying expedition, and required of those who en-

gaged in it to be so too. They cast a broad shadōw of thought and seriousness over the cause; and, if this sometimes deepened into melancholy and bitterness, can we find no apology for such a human weakness?

2. It is sad, indeed, to reflect on the disasters which the little band of Pilgrims encountered; sad to see a pōrtion of them, the prey of unrelenting cupidity, treacherously embarked in an unsound, unseaworthy ship, which they are soon oblīged to abandon, and crowd themselves into one vessel; one hundred persons, besides the ship's company, in a vessel of one hundred and sixty tons. One is touched at the stōry of the lŏng, cold, and weary autumnal passage; of the landing on the inhŏspital rocks at this dismal season; where they are deserted, before long, by the ship which had brought them, and which seemed their ōnly hold upon the world of fellōw-men, a prey to the elements and to want, and fearfully ignorant of the numbers, the power, and the temper of the savage tribes that filled the unexplōred continent upon whose verge they had ventured.

3. But all this wrought together for good. These trials of wandering and exile, of the ocean, the winter, the wilderness, and the savage foe, were the final assurances of success. It was these that put far away from our fathers' cause all patrician sŏftness, all hereditary claims to preëminence. No effeminate nobility crowded into the dark and austere ranks of the Pilgrims. No Carr nor Villers would lead on the ill-provided band of despised Puritans. No well-endowed clergy were on the alert to quit their cathedrals, and set up a pŏmpous hierarchy in the frozen wilderness. No craving governors were anxious to be sent over to our cheerless El Dorādos of ice and snow.

4. No; they could not say they had encouraged, patron-
ized, or helped the Pilgrims: their own cares, their own
labors, their own councils, their own blood, contrived all,
achieved all, bŏre all, sealed all. They could not after-
wards fairly pretend to·reap where they had not strewn;
and, as our fathers reared this broad and solid fabric with
pains and watchfulness, unaided, barely tolerated, it did
not fall when the favor, which had always been with-
holden, was changed into wrath; when the arm, which
had never supported, was raised to destroy.

5. Methinks I see it now, that one solitary, adventur-
ous vessel, the Mayflower of a forlorn hope, freighted
with the prospects of a future State, and bound ăcrŏss the
unknown sea. I behold it pursuing, with a thousand mis-
givings, the uncertain, the tedious voyage.___Suns rise
and set, and weeks and months pass, and winter surprises
them on the deep, but brings them not the sight of the
wished-for shŏre.

6. I see them now scantily supplied with provisions;
crowded almost to suffocation in their ill-stŏred prison;
delayed·by calms, pursuing a circuitous route—and now
driven in fury befŏre the raging tĕmpĕst, on the high
and giddy waves. The awful voice of the storm·howls
through the rigging. The laboring masts seem straining
from their base; the dismal sound of the pumps is
heard; the ship leaps, as it were, madly, from billŏw to
billow; the ocean breaks and settles with ingulfing floods
over the floating deck, and beats, with deadening, shivering weight, against the staggered vessel.

7. I see them, escaped from these perils, pursuing their
all but desperate undertaking, and landed at last, after a
five months' passage, on the ice-clad rocks of Plymouth—
weak and weary from the voyage, poorly armed, scantily

provisioned, depending on the charity of their shipmaster for a draught of beer on bōard, drinking nothing but water on shōre—without shelter, without means—surrounded by hŏstĭle tribes.

8. Shut now the volume of history, and tell me, on any principle of human probability, what shall be the fate of this handful of adventurers. Tell me, man of military science, in how many months were they all swept ŏff by the thirty savage tribes, enumerated within the early limits of New England? Tell me, politician, how lŏng dịd this shadōw of a colony, on which your conventions and treaties had not smiled, languish on the distant cōast? Student of history, compare for me the baffled prŏjects, the deserted settlements, the abandoned adventures of other times, and find the parallel of this.

9. Was it the winter's storm, beating upon the houseless heads of women and children; was it hard labor and spare meals; was it disease; was it the tomahawk; was it the deep malady of a blighted hope, a ruined enterprise, and a broken heart, aching in its last moments at the recollection of the loved and left beyŏnd the sea—was it some, or all of these united, that hŭrried this forsaken company to their melancholy fate; and is it possible that nēither of these causes, that not all combined were able to blast this bud of hope? Is it possible, that, from a beginning so feeble, so frail, so worthy, not so much of admiration as of pity, there has gŏne fōrth a prŏgress so steady, a growth so wonderful, an expansion so ample, a reälity so important, a promise, yĕt to be fulfilled, so glōrious?

EDWARD EVERETT.

MORNING.

Sweet is the breath of Morn, her rising sweet,
With charm of earliĕst birds; pleasant the sun,

When first on this delightful land he spreads
His orient beams, on *herb*, tree, fruit, and flower,
Glistening with dew; fragrant the fertile earth
After sŏft showers; and sweet the coming on
Of grateful evening mild: then silent Night,
With this her solemn bird, and this fair moon,
And these the gems of heaven, her starry train.

MILTON.

THE DILEMMA.—SCENE FROM PICKWICK.

Mr. Pickwick's apartments in Goswell street, although
on a limited scale, were not ōnly of a vĕry neat and com-
fortable description, but peculiarly adapted for the resi-
dence of a man of his genius and observation. His sĭt-
ting-room was the first floor front, his bed-roôm was the
second floor front; and thus, whether he was sitting at
his desk in the parlor, or standing befŏre the dressing-
glass in his dormitory, he had an equal opportunity of
contemplating human nature in all the numerous phases
it exhibits, in that not mōre populous than popular thor-
oughfare.

2. His landlady, Mrs. Bardell—the relict and sole ex-
ecutrix of a deceased custom-house ŏfficer—was a comely
(kŭm'ly) woman of bustling manners and agreeable appearance, with a natural genius for cooking, improved by
study and lōng practice into an ĕx'quĭsĭte talent. There
were no children, no servants, no fowls. The ōnly other
inmates of the house were a large man and a small boy;
the first a lodger, the second a production of Mrs. Bardell's. The large man was always at home precisely at
ten o'clock at night, at which hour he regularly con-
densed himself into the limits of a dwarfish French bed-
stead in the back parlor; and the infantine sports and
gymnastic exercises of Master Bardell were exclusively

confined to the neighboring pavements and gutters. Cleanliness and quiet reigned throughout the house; and in it Mr. Pickwick's will was law.

3. To any one acquainted with these points of the domestic economy of the establishment, and cŏn'versant with the admirable regulation of Mr. Pickwick's mind, his appearance and behavior, on the morning previous to that which had been fixed upon for the journey to Eatansvill, would have been mōst mysterious and unaccountable. He paced the room to and fro with hŭrried steps, popped his head out of the windōw at intervals of about three minutes each, constantly referred to his watch, and exhibited many other manifestations of impatience, vĕry unusual with him. It was evident that something of great importance was in contemplation; but what that something was, not even Mrs. Bardell herself had been enabled to discover.

4. "Mrs. Bardell," said Mr. Pickwick, at last, as that amiable female approached the termination of a prolonged dusting of the apartment. "Sir," said Mrs. Bardell. "Your little boy is a vĕry long time gone." "Why, it's a good long way to the Borough, sir," remonstrated Mrs. Bardell. "Ah," said Mr. Pickwick, "vĕry true; so it is." Mr. Pickwick relapsed into silence, and Mrs. Bardell resumed her dusting.

5. "Mrs. Bardell," said Mr. Pickwick, at the expiration of a few minutes. "Sir," said Mrs. Bardell again. "Do you think it's a much greater expense to keep two people, than to keep one?" "La, Mr. Pickwick," said Mrs. Bardell, coloring up to the vĕry border of her cap, as she fancied she observed a species of matrimonial twinkle in the eyes of her lodger; "La, Mr. Pickwick, what a question!" "Well, but *do* you?" inquired Mr. Pickwick. "That de-

4

pends," said Mrs. Bardell, approaching the duster very near to Mr. Pickwick's elbow, which was planted on the table; "that depends a good deal upon the person, you know, Mr. Pickwick; and whether it's a saving and careful person, sir." "That's very true," said Mr. Pickwick; "but the person I have in my eye (here he looked very hard at Mrs. Bardell) I think possesses these qualities; and has, moreover, a considerable knowledge of the world, and a great deal of sharpness, Mrs. Bardell; which may be of material use to me."

6. "La, Mr. Pickwick," said Mrs. Bardell; the crimson rising to her cap-border again. "I do," said Mr. Pickwick growing energetic, as was his wont (wŭnt) in speaking of a subject which interested him. "I do, indeed; and to tell you the truth, Mrs. Bardell, I have made up my mind." "Dear me, sir," exclaimed Mrs. Bardell. "You'll think it not very strange now," said the amiable Mr. Pickwick, with a good-humored glance at his companion, "that I never consulted you about this matter, and never mentioned it, till I sent your little boy out this morning—eh?"

7. Mrs. Bardell could only reply by a look. She had long worshipped Mr. Pickwick at a distance, but here she was, all at once, raised to a pinnacle to which her wildèst and mōst extravagant hopes had never dared to aspire. Mr. Pickwick was going to propose—a deliberate plan, too—sent her little boy to the Borough, to get him out of the way—how thoughtful—how considerate!—"Well," said Mr. Pickwick, "what do you think?" "Oh, Mr. Pickwick," said Mrs. Bardell, trembling with agitation, "you're věry kind, sir," "It will save you a great deal of trouble, wōn't it?" said Mr. Pickwick. "Oh, I never thought anything of the trouble, sir," replied Mrs. Bar-

dell; "and of course, I should take more trouble to please you than ever; but it is so kind of you, Mr. Pickwick, to have so much consideration for my loneliness."

8. "Ah, to be sure," said Mr. Pickwick; "I never thought of that. When I am in town, you'll always have somebody to sit with you. To be sure, so you will." "I am sure I ought to be a very happy woman," said Mrs. Bardell. "And your little boy—" said Mr. Pickwick. "Bless his heart," interposed Mrs. Bardell, with a maternal sob. "He, too, will have a companion," resumed Mr. Pickwick, "a lively one, who'll teach him, I'll be bound, more tricks in a week, than he would ever learn in a year." And Mr. Pickwick smiled placidly.

9. "Oh you dear—" said Mrs. Bardell. Mr. Pickwick started. "Oh you kind, good, playful dear," said Mrs. Bardell; and without more ado, she rose from her chair, and flung her arms round Mr. Pickwick's neck, with a cataract of tears, and a chorus of sobs. "Bless my soul," cried the astonished Mr. Pickwick;—"Mrs. Bardell, my good woman—dear me, what a situation—pray consider. Mrs. Bardell, don't—if anybody should come—" "Oh, let them come," exclaimed Mrs. Bardell, frantically; "I'll never leave you—dear, kind, good soul;" and, with these words, Mrs. Bardell clung the tighter.

10. "Mercy upon me," said Mr. Pickwick, struggling violently, "I hear somebody coming up the stairs. Don't, don't, there's a good creature, don't." But entreaty and remonstrance were alike unavailing: for Mrs. Bardell had fainted in Mr. Pickwick's arms; and before he could gain time to deposit her on a chair, Master Bardell entered the room, ushering in Mr. Tupman, Mr. Winkle, and Mr. Snodgrass. Mr. Pickwick was struck motionless and speechless. He stood with his lovely burden in

his arms, gazing vacantly on the countenances of his friends, without the slightest attempt at recognition or explanation. They, in their turn, stared at him; and Master Bardell, in his turn, stared at everybody.

11. The astonishment of the Pickwickians was so absorbing, and the perplexity of Mr. Pickwick was so extreme, that they might have remained in exactly the same relative situation until the suspended animation of the lady was restored, had it not been for a most beautiful and touching expression of filial affection on the part of her youthful son. Clad in a tight suit of corduroy, spangled with brass-buttons of a very considerable size, he at first stood at the door astounded and uncertain; but by degrees, the impression that his mother must have suffered some personal damage, pervaded his partially developed mind, and considering Mr. Pickwick the aggressor, he set up an appalling and semi-earthly kind of howling, and butting forward, with his head, commenced assailing that immortal gentleman about the back and legs, with such blows and pinches as the strength of his arm and the violence of his excitement allowed.

12. "Take this little villain away," said the agonized Mr. Pickwick, "he's mad." "What *is* the matter?" said the three tongue-tied Pickwickians. "I don't know," replied Mr. Pickwick, pettishly. "Take away the boy—(here Mr. Winkle carried the interesting boy, screaming and struggling, to the farther end of the apartment). Now help me to lead this woman down stairs." "Oh, I'm better now," said Mrs. Bardell, faintly. "Let me lead you down stairs," said the ever gallant Mr. Tupman. "Thank you, sir—thank you;" exclaimed Mrs. Bardell, hysterically. And down stairs she was led accordingly, accompanied by her affectionate son.

13. "I can not conceive"—said Mr. Pickwick, when his friend returned—"I can not conceive what has been the matter with that woman. I had merely announced to her my intention of keeping a man-servant, when she fell into the extraordinary paroxysm in which you found her. Vĕry extraordinary thing." "Very," said his three friends. "Placed me in such an extremely awkward situation,"—continued Mr. Pickwick. "Very;" was the reply of his followers, as they coughed slightly, and looked dubiously at each other.

14. This behavior was not lost upon Mr. Pickwick. He remarked their incredulity. They evidently suspected him. "There is a man in the passage now," said Mr. Tupman. "It's the man that I spoke to you about," said Mr. Pickwick, "I sent for him to the Borough this morning. Have the goodness to call him up, Mr. Snodgrass." DICKENS.

DEITY.

1. A million torches, lighted by Thy hand,
Wander unwearied through the blue abyss—
They own Thy power, accomplish Thy command,
All gay with life, all eloquent with bliss.
What shall we call them? Piles of crystal light—
A glŏrious company of golden streams—
Lamps of celestial ether burning bright—
Suns lighting systems with their joyous beams?
But Thou to these art as the noon to night.

2. Yĕs! as a drop of water in the sea,
All this magnificence in Thee is lost:—
What are ten thousand worlds compared to Thee?
And what am I then?—Heaven's unnumbered host,
Though multiplied by myriads, and arrayed
In all the glŏry of sublimĕst thought,
Is but an atom in the balance, weighed

Against Thy greatness—is a cipher brought
Against infinity! What am I then? Naught!

3. Naught! But the effluence of Thy light divine,
Pervading worlds, hath reached my bosom too;
Yĕs! In my spirit doth Thy spirit shine
As shines the sun-beam in a drop of dew.
Naught! but I live, and on hope's pinions fly
Eager toward Thy presence; for in Thee
I live, and breathe, and dwell; aspiring high.

4. Thou art!—directing, guiding all—Thou art!
Direct my understanding then to Thee;
Control my spirit, guide my wandering heart;
Though but an atom 'midst immensity,
Still I am something, fashioned by Thy hand!
I hold a middle rank 'twixt heaven and earth—
On the last verge of mortal being stand,
Close to the realms where angels have their birth,
Just on the boundaries of the spirit-land!

5. The chain of being is complete in me—
In me is matter's last gradation lost,
And the next step is spirit—Deity!
I can command the lightning, and am dust!
A monarch and a slave—a worm, a god!
Whence came I here, and how? so marvelously
Constructed and conceived? unknown! this clod
Lives surely through some higher energy;
For from itself alone it could not be!

6. Creator, yĕs! Thy wisdom and Thy word
Created me! Thou sōurce of life and good!
Thou spirit of my spirit, and my Lord!
Thy light, Thy love, in their bright plenitude
Filled me with an immortal soul, to spring
Over the abyss of death; and bắde it wear
The garments of eternal day, and wing
Its heavenly flight beyŏnd this little sphere,
Even to its sōurce—to Thee—its Author there.

7. O thoughts ineffable! O visions blest!
  Though worthless our conceptions all of Thee,
  Yĕt shall Thy shadōwed image fill our breast,
  And waft its homage to Thy Deity.
  Gŏd! thus ălōne my lowly thoughts can sōar,
  Thus seek Thy presence—Being wise and good!
  'Midst Thy vast works admire, obey, ădōre;
  And when the tongue is eloquent no mōre
  The soul shall speak in tears of gratitude.

DERZHAVEN.

THE DEATH OF HAMILTON.

A short time since, and he, who is the occasion of our sŏrrōws, was the ornament of his country. He stood on an eminence, and glōry covered him. From that eminence he has fallen: suddenly, forever fallen. His intercōurse with the living world is now ended; and those who would hereafter find him, must seek him in the grave. There, cold and lifèless, is the heart which just now was the seat of friendship; there, dim and sightless, is the eye, whose rādiant and enlivening orb beamed with intelligence; and there, closed forever, are those lips, on whose persuasive accents we have so ŏften, and so lately hung with transpōrt!

2. From the darkness which rests upon his tomb there proceeds, methinks, a light, in which it is clearly seen, that those gaudy objects which men pursue are ōnly phantoms. In this light how dimly shines the splendor of victory—how humble appears the majesty of grandeur! The bubble, which seemed to have so much solidity, has burst: and we again see, that all below the sun is vanity!

3. True, the funeral eulogy has been pronounced, the sad and solemn procession has moved, the badge of mōurn-

ing has already been decreed, and presently the sculptured marble will lift up its front, proud to perpetuate the name of Hamilton, and rehearse to the passing traveler his virtues (just tributes of respect, and to the living useful); but to him, moldering in his narrow and humble habitation, what are they? How vain! how unavailing!

4. Approach, and behold, while I lift from his sepulchre its covering! Ye admirers of his greatness! ye emulous of his talents and his fame! approach and behold him now. How pale! how silent! No martial bands admire the adroitness of his movements; no fascinating throng weep, and melt, and tremble at his eloquence! Amazing change! a shroud! a coffin! a narrow, subterraneous cabin!—this is all that now remains of Hamilton! And is this all that remains of Hamilton? During a life so transitory, what lasting monument, then, can our fondest hopes erect!

5. My brethren, we stand on the borders of an awful gulf, which is swallowing up all things human. And is there, amidst this universal wreck, nothing stable, nothing abiding, nothing immortal, on which poor, frail, dying man can fasten? Ask the hero, ask the statesman, whose wisdom you have been accustomed to revere, and he will tell you: He will tell you, did I say? He has already told you, from his death-bed; and his illumined spirit still whispers from the heavens, with well-known eloquence, the solemn admonition: "Mortals hastening to the tomb, and once the companions of my pilgrimage, take warning and avoid my errors; cultivate the virtues I have recommended; choose the Saviour I have chosen; live disinterestedly; live for immortality; and would you rescue any thing from final dissolution, lay it up in God."

NOTT.

THE STARS.

Roll on, ye stars; exult in youthful prime;
Mark with bright curves the printless steps of Time;
Near and more near your beamy cars approach,
And lessening orbs on lessening orbs encroach.
Flowers of the sky, ye, too, to age must yield,
Frail as your silken sisters of the field.

Star after star from heaven's high arch shall rush,
Suns sink on suns, and systems systems crush,
Headlong, extinct, to one dark centre fall,
And death, and night, and chaos mingle all;
Till o'er the wreck, emerging from the storm,
Immortal Nature lifts her changeful form,
Mounts from her funeral pyre, on wings of flame,
And soars and shines, another and the same.

DARWIN.

PUBLIC VIRTUE.

1. I hope, that in all that relates to personal firmness, all that concerns a just appreciation of the insignificance of human life,—whatever may be attempted to threaten or alarm a soul not easily swayed by opposition, or awed or intimidated by menace,—a stout heart and a steady eye, that can survey', unmoved and undaunted, any mere personal perils that assail this poor, transient, perishing frame, —I may, without disparagement, compare with other men.

2. But there is a sort of courage, which, I frankly confess it, I do not possess,—a boldness to which I dare not aspire, a valor which I can not covet.. I can not lay myself down in the way of the welfare and happiness of my country. That I can not, I have not the courage to do.

I can not interpose the power with which I may be invested—a power conferred, not for my personal benefit, nor for my aggrăn'dĭzement, but for my country's good—to check her onward march to greatness and glŏry. I have not courage enough. I am too cowardly for that.

3. I would not, I dare not, in the exercise of such a trust, lie down, and place my body ăcrŏss the path that leads my country to prosperity and happiness. This is a sort of coŭrage widely different from that which a man may display in his private conduct and personal relations. Personal or private courage is totally distinct from that higher and nobler courage which prŏmpts the pātriot to ŏffer himself a voluntary săcrifice to his country's good.

4. Apprehensions of the imputation of the want of firmness sometimes impel us to perform rash and inconsiderate acts. It is the greatest coŭrage to be able to bear the imputation of the want of courage. But pride, vanity, ēgotism, so unamiable and offensive in private life, are vices which partake of the character of crimes, in the conduct of public affairs. The unfortunate victim of these passions can not see beyŏnd the little, petty, contemptible circle of his own personal ĭnterĕsts. All his thoughts are withdrawn from his country, and concentrated on his consistency, his firmness, himself.

5. The high, the exalted, the sublime emotions of a pātriotism, which, sŏaring toward heaven, rises far above all mean, low, or selfish things, and is absorbed by one soul-transpŏrting thought of the good and the glŏry of one's country, are never felt in his impenetrable bosom. That patriotism, which, cătching its inspirations from the immortal Gŏd, and leaving at an imměasurable distance below all lesser, grŏveling, personal interests and feelings, animates and prŏmpts to deeds of self-săcrifice, of valor,

of devotion, and of death itself,—that is public virtue; that is the noblest, the sublimest, of all public virtues.

H. CLAY.

CRITICISM.

WHOEVER thinks a faultless piece to see
Thinks what ne'er was, nor is, nor e'er shall be.
In every work regard the writer's end,
Since none can compass more than they intend ;
And, if the means be just, the conduct true,
Applause, in spite of trivial faults, is due..
As men of breeding; sometimes men of wit,
To avoid great errors must the less commit;
Neglect the rules each verbal critic lays;
For not to know some trifles, is a praise.
Most critics, fond of some subservient art,
Still make the whole depend upon a part:
They talk of principles, but notions prize;
And all to one loved folly sacrifice. POPE.

THE REVOLUTIONARY ALARM.

DARKNESS closed upon the country and upon the town, but it was no night for sleep. Heralds on swift relays of horses transmitted the war-message from hand to hand, till village repeated it to village; the sea to the backwoods; the plains to the highlands; and it was never suffered to droop; till it had been borne North, and South, and East, and West, throughout the land.

2. It spread over the bays that receive the Saco and the Penobscot. Its loud reveille broke the rest of the trappers of New Hampshire, and ringing like bugle-notes from peak to peak, overleapt the Green Mountains, swept onward to Montreal, and descended the ocean river, till the responses were echoed from the cliffs of Quebec. The hills along the Hudson told to one another the tale.

3. As the summons hurried to the South, it was one day at New York; in one more at Philadelphia; the next it lighted a watchfire at Baltimore; thence it waked an answer at Annapolis. Crossing the Potomac near Mount Vernon, it was sent forward without a halt to Williamsburg. It traversed the Dismal Swamp to Nansemond, along the route of the first emigrants to North Carolina. It moved onwards and still onwards through boundless groves of evergreen to Newbern and to Wilmington.

4. " For God's sake forward it by night and by day," wrote Cornelius Harnett, by the express which sped for Brunswick. Patriots of South Carolina caught up its tones at the border and despatched it to Charleston, and through pines and palmetos and moss-clad live oaks, further to the South, till it resounded among the New England settlements beyond the Savannah.

5. The Blue ridge took up the voice and made it heard from one end to the other of the valley of Virginia. The Alleghanies, as they listened, opened their barriers that the "loud call" might pass through to the hardy riflemen on the Holston, the Watauga, and the French Broad. Ever renewing its strength, powerful enough even to create a commonwealth, it breathed its inspiring word to the first settlers of Kentucky; so that hunters who made their halt in the machless valley of the Elkhorn, commemorated the 19th day of April, 1776, by naming their encampment *Lexington*.

6. With one impulse the colonies sprung to arms; with one spirit they pledged themselves to each other "to be ready for the extreme event." With one heart the continent cried, "LIBERTY OR DEATH."

BANCROFT.

SHERIDAN'S RIDE.

1. Up from the South at break of dāy,
   Bringing to Winchester fresh dismāy,
   The affrighted air with a shudder bōre,
   Like a herald in haste, to the chieftain's dōor,
   The terrible grumble, and rumble, and rŏar,
   Telling the battle was on once mōre,
   And Sheridan—twenty miles ăwāy.

2. And wider still those billōws of war
   Thundered ălŏng the horī'zon's bar,
   And louder yĕt into Winchester rolled
   The rōar of that red sea uncontrolled,
   Making the blood of the listener cold
   As he thought of the stake in that fiery fray,
   And Sheridan—twenty miles away.

3. But there is a rōad from Winchester town,
   A good, broad highway leading down;
   And there, through the flush of the morning light,
   A steed, as black as the steeds of night,
   Was seen to pass as with eagle flight—
   As if he knew the terrible need,
   He stretched away with the utmost speed;
   Hills rose and fell—but his heart was gay,
   With Sheridan fifteen miles away.

4. Still sprung from these swift hoofs, thundering South,
   The dust, like the smoke from the cannon's mouth,
   Or the trail of a comet sweeping faster and faster,
   Foreboding to foemen the doom of disaster;
   The heart of the steed and the heart of the master
   Were beating like prisoners assaulting their walls,
   Impatient to be where the battle-field calls ;
   Every nerve of the charger was strained to full play,
   With Sheridan only ten miles away.

5. Under his spurning feet, the rōad
   Like an ărrōwy Al'pine river flōwed,

And the landscape sped away behind
Like an ocean flying before the wind;
And the steed, like a bark fed with furnace ire,
Swept on with his wild eyes full of fire.
But, lo! he is nearing his heart's desire—
He is snuffing the smoke of the roaring fray,
With Sheridan only five miles away.

6. The first that the General saw were the groups
Of stragglers, and then the retreating troops;—
What was done—what to do—a glance told him both,
Then striking his spurs with a terrible oath,
He dashed down the line 'mid a storm of huzzahs,
And the wave of retreat checked its course there because
The sight of the master compelled it to pause.
With foam and with dust the black charger was gray;
By the flash of his eye, and his red nostril's play,
He seemed to the whole great army to say, ——
"I have brought you Sheridan all the way
From Winchester down to save the day!"

7. Hurrah, hurrah for Sheridan!
Hurrah, hurrah for horse and man!
And when their statues are placed on high
Under the dome of the Union sky,—
The American soldier's Temple of Fame,—
There, with the glorious General's name,
Be it said in letters both bold and bright:
"Here is the steed that saved the day
By carrying Sheridan into the fight
From Winchester—twenty miles away!"

T. B. REED.

THE RAVEN.

1.

ONCE upon a midnight dreary, while I pondered, weak and
    weary,
Over many a quaint and curious volume of forgotten lore—

While I nodded, nearly napping, suddenly there came a tap-
ping,
As of some one gently rapping, rapping at my chāmber-door.
" 'Tis some visitor," I muttered, "tapping at my chamber-
door—
Only this, and nothing more."

2.

Ah, distinctly I remember, it was in the bleak December,
And each separate dying ember wrought its ghost upon the
floor,
Eagerly I wished the mŏrrŏw: vainly I had sought to bŏrrŏw
From my books surcease of sŏrrŏw—sorrow for the lŏst
Lenōre—
For the rare and rādiant maiden whom the āngels name
Lenore—
Nameless here forĕvermōre.

3.

And the silken, sad, uncertain rustling of each purple curtain,
Thrilled me—filled me with fantastic terrors never felt before;
So that now, to still the beating of my heart, I stood repeat-
ing,
" 'Tis some visitor entreating entrance at my chāmber-dōor,—
Some late visitor entreating entrance at my chamber-door—
That it is, and nothing more."

4.

Presently my soul grew strŏnger: hesitating then no lŏnger,
" Sir," said I, " or Madam, truly your forgiveness I implōre;
But the fact is, I was napping, and so gently you came rap-
ping,
And so faintly you came tapping, tapping at my chāmber-
door,
That I scarce was sure I heard you"—here I opened wide the
door,—
Darkness there, and nothing more.

5.

Deep into that darkness peering, lŏng I stood there wonder-
    ing, fearing,
Doubting, dreaming dreams no mortals ever dared to dream
    before;
But the silence was unbroken, and the stillness gave no token,
And the ŏnly word there spoken was the whispered word
    "Lenore!"
This *I* whisper'd, and an echo murmured back the word,
    "LENORE!"
        Merely this, and nothing more.

6.

Back into the chămber turning, all my soul within me burn-
    ing,
Soon again I heard a tapping, someting louder than before.
"Surely," said I, "surely that is something at my windŏw-
    lattice;
Let me see then what thereat is, and this mystery explŏre,—
Let my heart be still a moment, and this mystery explore;—
        'Tis the wind, and nothing mŏre."

7.

Open here I flung the shutter, when, with many a flirt and
    flutter,
In there stepped a stately raven of the stately days of yŏre.
Not the least obĕisance made he; not a minute stopp'd or
    stay'd he;
But, with mien of lord or lady, perch'd above my chămber-
    door,—
Perch'd upon a bust of Pallas, just above my chamber-door—
        Perch'd, and sat, and nothing more.

8.

Then this ebony bird beguiling my sad fancy into smiling,
By the grave and stern decŏrum of the countenance it wŏre,

"Though thy crest be shōrn and shaven, thou," I said, "art sure no craven;
Ghastly, grim, and ancient raven, wandering from the nightly shōre,
Tell me what thy lordly name is on the Night's Plutonian shore ?"
Quoth the raven, "Nevermore!"

9.

Much I marveled this ungainly fowl to hear discōurse so plainly,
Though its answer little meaning—little relevancy bōre;
For we can not help agreeing that no living human being
Ever yĕt was blessed with seeing bird above his chămber-door—
Bird or beast upon the sculptured bust above his chamber-door,
With such name as "Nevermore!"

10.

But the raven sitting lonely on the placid bust, spoke ōnly
That one word, as if his soul in that one word he did outpōur.
Nothing further then he utter'd—not a feather then he flutter'd—
Till I scarcely more than mutter'd, "Other friends have flown before—
On the mŏrrŏw *he* will leave me, as my hopes have flown before."
Then the bird said, "Nevermore!"

11.

Startled at the stillness, broken by reply so aptly spoken,
"Doubtless," said I, "what it utters is its only stock and stōre,
Caught from some unhappy master, whom unmerciful disaster
Follōw'd fast and follow'd faster, till his sŏngs one burden bōre,—
Till the dirges of his hope that melancholy burden bore,
Of—"Never—nevermore!"

12.

But the raven still beguiling all my sad soul into smiling,
Straight I wheeled a cushioned seat in front of bird, and bust,
    and door,
Then, upon the velvet sinking, I betook myself to linking
Fancy unto fancy, thinking what this ominous bird of yōre—
What this grim, ungainly, ghastly, gaunt, and ominous bird
    of yore
            Meant in croaking "Nevermore!"

13.

This I sat engaged in guessing, but no syllable expressing
To the fowl, whose fiery eyes now burned into my bosom's
    cōre;
This and mōre I sat dīvīning, with my head at ease reclining
On the cushion's velvet lining that the lamp-light glōated
    ō'er,
But whose velvet violet lining, with the lamp-light gloating
    o'er,
            She shall press—ah! nevermore!

14.

Then methought the air grew denser, perfumed from an un-
    seen censer
Swung by seraphim, whose foot-falls tinkled on the tufted
    floor.
"Wretch," I cried, "thy Gŏd hath lent thee—by these āngels
    he hath sent thee
Respite—respite and nepenthe from thy memories of Lenore!
Quaff, oh, quaff this kind nepenthe, and forgĕt this lŏst
    Lenore!"
            Quoth the raven, "Nevermore!"

15.

"Prophet!" said I, "thing of evil!—prophet still, if bird or
    devil!
Whether tempter sent, or whether tempest tŏss'd thee here
    ăshōre,

Desolate, yĕt all undaunted, on this desert land enchanted—
On this home by Hŏrror haunted—tell me truly, I implōre—
Is there—*is* there balm in Gilead?—tell me—tell me, I im-
    plore!"
        Quoth the raven, "Nevermore!"

16.

"Prophet!" said I, "thing of evil!—prophet still, if bird or
    devil!
By that heaven that bends above us—by that God we both
    ădōre,
Tell this soul, with sŏrrŏw laden, if, within the distant
    Aidenn,
It shall clasp a sainted maiden, whom the āngels name Lenōre;
Clasp a rare and rādient maiden, whom the angels name
    Lenore—
        Quoth the raven, "Nevermore!"

17.

"Be that word our sign of parting, bird or fiend!" I shrieked,
    upstarting—
"Gĕt thee back into the tempest and the Night's Plutonian
    shōre!
Leave no black plume as a token of that lie thy soul hath
    spoken!
Leave my loneliness unbroken!—quit the bust above my
    dōor!
Take thy bĕak from out my heart, and take thy form from
    ŏff my door!"
        Quoth the raven, "Nevermore!"

18.

And the raven, never flitting, still is sitting, still is sitting
On the pallid bust of Pallas, just above my chamber-door;
And his eyes have all the seeming of a dĕmon's that is dream-
    ing,
And the lamp-light o'er him streaming throws his shădōw on
    the floor;

And my soul from out that shadow that lies floating on the
floor
   Shall be lifted—NEVERMORE!

         EDGAR A. POE.

THE BELLS.

HEAR the sledges with the bells—
 Silver bells—
What a world or merriment their melody foretells!
 How they tinkle, tinkle, tinkle,
  In the icy air of night!
 While the stars that oversprinkle
 All the heavens, seem to twinkle
  With a crystalline delight;
 Keeping time, time, time,
 In a sort of Runic rhyme,
To the tintinnabulation that so musically wells
 From the bells, bells, bells, bells,
  Bells, bells, bells—
From the jingling and the tinkling of the bells.

2.

 Hear the mellow wedding-bells,
  Golden bells!
What a world of happiness their harmony foretells!
 Through the balmy air of night
 How they ring out their delight!
 From the molten-golden notes,
  And all in tune,
 What a liquid ditty floats
To the turtle-dove that listens, while she gloats
  On the moon!
 Oh, from out the sounding cells,
What a gush of euphony voluminously wells!
  How it swells!
  How it dwells
 On the Future! how it tells
 Of the rapture that impels

To the swinging and the ringing
Of the bells, bells, bells—
Of the bells, bells, bells, bells,
Bells, bells, bells—
To the rhyming and the chiming of the bells!

3

Hear the loud alarum bells—
Brazen bells!
What a tale of těrror, now, their turbulency tells!
In the startled ear of night
How they scream out their affright!
Too much hŏrrifled to speak,
They can only shriek, shriek,
Out of tune,
In a clamorous appealing to the mercy of the fire,
In a mad expostulation with the děaf and frantic fire
Leaping higher, higher, higher,
With a desperate desire
And a resolute endeavor,
Now—now to sit or never,
By the side of the pale-faced moon.
Oh, the bells, bells, bells!
What a tale their terror tells
Of despair!
How they clang, and clash, and rōar!
What a hŏrror they outpŏur
On the bosom of the palpitating air!
Yět the air, it fully knows,
By the twanging
And the clanging,
How the dănger ebbs and flows;
Yet the ear distinctly tells
In the jangling
And the wrangling,
How the danger sinks and swells,
By the sinking or the swelling in the anger of the bells—
Of the bells—

Of the bells, bells, bells, bells,,
    Bells, bells, bells—
In the clamor and the clangor of the bells!

4.

    Hear the tŏlling of the bells—
        Iron bells!
What a world of solemn thought their monody compels!
     In the silence of the night,
     How we shiver with affright
At the mĕl'ancholy menace of their tōne!
     For every sound that flōats
     From the rust within their throats
        Is a grōan.
     And the people—ah, the people—
     They that dwell up in the steeple,
        All ălōne,
    And who tŏlling, tŏlling, tŏlling,
       In that muffled monotone,
     Feel a glōry in so rōlling
       On the human heart a stone—
     They are nĕither man nor woman—
     They are neither brute nor human—
        They are Ghouls:
     And their king it is who tŏlls;
     And he rŏlls, rolls, rolls, rolls,
        A pæan from the bells!
     And his mĕrry bosom swells
       With the pæan of the bells!
     And he dances and he yells;
     Keeping time, time, time,
     In a sort of Runic rhyme,
       To the pæan of the bells—
        Of the bells:
     Keeping time, time, time,
     In a sort of Runic rhyme,
       To the throbbing of the bells—
     Of the bells, bells, bells,
       To the sobbing of the bells;

Keeping time, time, time,
  As he knells, knells, knells,
In a happy Runic rhyme,
  To the rolling of the bells—
Of the bells, bells, bells—
  To the tolling of the bells,
Of the bells, bells, bells, bells,.
  Bells, bells, bells—
To the moaning and the groaning of the bells.

EDGAR A. POE.

The preceding pieces—"Sheridan's Ride," "The Raven," and "The Bells," are the three most popular in our language, either for private exercise or public declamation. Indeed, any one who can speak them *well* will have little difficulty with ordinary compositions.

CHRISTMAS.

RING out, wild bells, to the wild sky,
  The flying cloud, the frosty light,
  The year is dying with the night;
Ring out, wild bells, and let him die.

Ring out the old, ring in the new,
  Ring happy bells across the snow;
  The year is going, let it go;
Ring out the false, ring in the true.

Ring out the grief that saps the mind,
  For those that here we see no more;
  Ring out the feud of rich and poor,
Ring in redress for all mankind.

Ring out a slowly, dying cause,
  And ancient forms of petty strife;
  Ring in the nobler modes of life,
With sweeter manners, purer laws.

Ring out the want, the woe, the sin,
   The faithless coldness of the times;
Ring out, ring out my mournful rhymes,
But ring the fuller minstrel in.

Ring out false pride in place and blood,
   The civic slander and the spite;
Ring in the love of truth and right,
Ring in the common love of good.

Ring out old shapes of foul disease,
   Ring out the narrowing lust of gold;
Ring out the thousand woes of old,
Ring in the thousand years of peace.

Ring in the valiant man and free,
   The larger heart, the kindlier hand;
Ring out the darkness of the land,
Ring in the CHRIST that is to be.

                         TENNYSON.

THE TOMAHAWK SUBMISSIVE TO ELOQUENCE.

1. TWENTY tomahawks were raised; twenty ărrŏws drawn to their head. Yĕt stood Harold stern and collected, at bay—parleying ōnly with his swōrd. He waved his arm. Smitten with a sense of their cow′ardĭce, perhaps, or by his great dignity, mōre awful for his vĕry youth, their wĕapons dropped, and their countenances were uplifted upon him, less in hatred than in wonder.

2. The old men găthered about him: he leaned upon his saber. Their eyes shōne with admiration : such heroic depōrtment, in one so young—a boy! so intrĕpid! so prŏmpt! so graceful! so eloquent, too!—for, knowing the effect of eloquence, and feeling the lŏftiness of his own nature, the innocence of his own heart, the character of the Indians for hŏspităl′ity, and their veneration for his

blood, Harold dealt out the thunder of his strength to these rude barbarians of the wilderness, till they, young and old, gathering nearer and nearer in their devotion, threw down their wĕapons at his feet, and formed a rampart of locked arms and hearts about him, through which his eloquence thrilled and lightened like electricity. The old greeted him with a lofty step, as the pātriarch welcomes his boy from the triumph of far-ŏff battle; and the young clave to him and clung to him, and shouted in their self-abandonment, like brothers round a conquering brother.

3. "Warriors!" he said, "Brethren!"—(their tomahawks were brandished sīmultā'neously, at the sound of his terrible voice, as if preparing for the onset). His tones grew deeper, and less threatening. "Brothers! let us talk togĕther of Logan! Ye who have known him, ye agèd men! bear ye testimony to the deeds of his strength. Who was like him? Who could resist him? Who may ăbĭde the hŭrricane in its volley? Who may withstand the winds that uproot the great trees of the mountain?. Let him be the foe of Logan. Thrice in one day hath he given battle. Thrice in one day hath he come back victorious. Who may bear up against the strong man—the man of war? Let them that are young, hear me. Let them follōw the cōurse of Logan. He goes in clouds and whirlwind—in the fire and in the smoke. Let them follow him. Warriors! Logan was the father of Harold!" They fell back in astonishment, but they believed him; for Harold's word was unquestioned, undoubted evidence, to them that knew him.   NEAL.

CHAPTER VIII.

ALL persons who participate in public meetings or debating societies, should make themselves acquainted with the established methods for conducting them. Without a strict adherence to certain recognized rules, it is impossible to avoid confusion and unprofitable wordy controversy. Referring the reader who desires to to be familiar with parliamentary usages in all their applications to "Cushing's Manual," "The American Debater," "The Normal Debater," and similar works, the chapter on this subject will be limited to the necessary rules for managing ordinary Lyceums and debating clubs; and as the Lyceum department of the Hygeio-Therapeutic College has been in existence for more than twenty years, and has simplified its organization to a good, if not the best, working condition, its constitution and by-laws will be presented as a chart or guide for others. This Lyceum has also an uncommon, if not peculiar, feature, which I would strongly commend to all Lyceums whose members are not accomplished speakers. It devotes one whole evening to the discussion of a question agreed on, and another evening to criticisms, readings, essays, and declamations, and so alternately. But, whether this last-named feature is adopted or not; its constitution and by-laws are equally applicable.

(98)

CONSTITUTION.

ARTICLE 1.—NAME.

This Association shall be entitled, The Hygeio-Therapeutic College Lyceum.

ARTICLE 2.—OBJECTS.

The objects of this Lyceum are, the mutual improvement of its members, and the investigation, in the spirit of candor and truth-seeking, of all problems that concern the welfare of human beings.

ARTICLE 3.—MEMBERSHIP.

Any person may become a member of this Lyceum, on receiving the affirmative vote of two-thirds of the members present at any regular meeting, and signing this Constitution.

ARTICLE 4.—EXPULSION.

Any member of this Lyceum may be expelled for grossly improper conduct, by a vote of two-thirds of the members present at any regular meeting.

ARTICLE 5.—OFFICERS.

The officers of this Lyceum shall consist of a President, Secretary, and Treasurer, who shall exercise their respective duties for one week, and until others are chosen to succeed them.*

ARTICLE 6.—AMENDMENTS.

This Constitution may be amended at any time by a vote of two-thirds of the members present at any regular

* A Corresponding Secretary should be elected when the proceedings of the Society require letter writing and the circulation of documents.

meeting, provided that notice has been given of the proposed amendment at a preceding regular meeting.

BY-LAWS.

1. MEETINGS.

The Lyceum shall meet in the Lecture Hall of the Hygeio-Therapeutic College, on Monday and Wedsesday evenings, at seven o'clock, and adjourn at nine o'clock.

2. QUORUM.

Five members shall constitute a quorum for the transaction of business. Any number of members less than a quorum may adjourn to the time of the next regular meeting.

3. ORDER OF BUSINESS.

The order of business on Monday evenings shall be :

a. Reading, correction, and adoption of the minutes.
b. Reception of new members.
c. Discussion of the question.
d. Adjournment.

On Wednesday evenings the order of business shall be :

a. Reception of new members.
b. Report of the critic.
c. Criticisms of the critic.
d. Readings, essays, and declamations.
e. Selection of question for debate.
f. Appointments.
g. Unfinished business.
h. New business.
i. Adjournment.

4. DUTIES OF OFFICERS.

The President shall occupy the chair, maintain the order of proceedings, decide all questions of parliamentary usage subject to appeal to the house, appoint all committees, critics, and leading disputants not otherwise provided for, give the casting vote in cases of a tie, and have charge of the books and papers of the Lyceum. The Secretary shall record its proceedings at each meeting, and report the same to the meetings on Monday evenings. The Treasurer shall have charge of the moneys and properties of the Lyceum.

5. APPOINTEES.

On each Wednesday evening a critic, reader, essayist, and declaimer shall be appointed for the ensuing Wednesday evening, and two leading disputants for the discussion on the ensuing Monday evening.*

6. SELECTION OF QUESTION.

The subject for debate shall be selected by a majority vote. Any member may propose, orally or in writing, a question or resolution for discussion.

7. CRITICISMS.

It shall be the duty of the critic to notice all errors in manner, gesture, pronunciation, and grammar, of the preceding meetings, and report the same. After the report of the critic is made, it shall be the privilege of any member to criticise the criticisms of the critic.

* When a Lyceum (as in this case) is composed of ladies and gentlemen, it is proper, when practicable, to appoint a lady to open the debate on one side, and a gentleman on the other.

Committees of more than one should be composed of both sexes.

8. LIMITATION OF SPEAKERS.

The leading disputants shall each be entitled to ten minutes to open, and five minutes to close the debate. All other speakers shall be limited to five minutes. The Lyceum may, at any time, by majority vote, extend the time of any speaker, but not exceeding five minutes.

9. ORDER OF DEBATE.

The affirmative and negative shall be represented alternately from the commencement to the close of the discussion. After the leading disputants have opened the debate, the members shall proceed with the discussion *pro* and *con*, in the order of their names on the book of the Secretary, unless one declines speaking, when the next in order shall be called. If no one offers to controvert the last speaker, another speech on the same side is in order. When all the members who desire to speak have been called, voluntary speakers, *pro* and *con*, may be called for; and if more than one rises to speak, the President shall decide, without appeal or debate, who is entitled to the floor. No one shall be permitted to speak twice until all have spoken who desire to do so, unless by unanimous consent.

POINTS OF ORDER.

All points of order, on being distinctly stated, shall be decided without debate. If the decision of the President is appealed from, the motion, "Shall the decision of the Chair be sustained?" shall be put and decided by a majority vote.

11. MANNER OF VOTING.

Voting may be done by ayes and noes, or by raising the hand, as the Chair shall determine. When the vote is doubtful or disputed, any member may call for a division of the house, when the vote shall be taken by rising or the uplifted hand, the President directing the Secretary to count the ayes and noes.

12. SUSPENSIONS.

Any by-law may be suspended for the evening by a vote of two-thirds of the members present; or it may be suspended indefinitely by unanimous consent.

13. AMENDMENTS.

These by-laws may be amended at any regular meeting of the Lyceum by a vote of two-thirds of the members present; or by a majority vote after one week's notice has been given.

PARLIAMENTARY USAGES.

1. *Motions.*—No motion can be entertained until seconded. When a motion is made and seconded, the President should rise, state the question fully and clearly, and ask if the house is ready for the question. If no one offers to speak, the motion should be put to vote, the result announced, and the Secretary directed to record it.

2. *Motions to Reconsider.*—A motion to reconsider cannot be entertained unless made and seconded by persons who voted with the majority, except in the case of an equal division, when it must be made by one who voted in the negative. No motion to reconsider is in order after the proposition or action has passed out of the possession of the house, or recorded and approved in the minutes.

3. *Motions to Expunge.*—Motions to expunge or rescind any resolution or vote of the house, require unanimous consent.

4. *Motions not Debatable.*—The previous or main question, points of order, motions to reconsider, to adjourn, and to lie on the table, are not debatable; nor are appeals from the decision of the Chair. But when two or more members make an appeal, the President may give his reasons for the decision, and the question may then be debated. In case of a tie vote, the President may give the casting vote in favor of his decision.

5. *The Previous Question.*—The previous question shall not be entertained unless the motion is seconded by three members. If the question is decided affirmatively, and amendments are pending, the vote should be taken first on the amendments in order, and then on the main question. All incidental questions arising after the previous question has been moved, must be decided without debate. When the previous question has been moved and seconded, it cannot be withdrawn without the consent of a majority; nor can it be suspended by any motion except that to adjourn.

6. *Amendments.*—An amendment to a pending motion is always in order; and so is an amendment to an amendment; but an amendment to an amendment cannot be amended. After the discussion the vote is to be taken, first on the amendment to the amendment, then on the amendment, and lastly on the main question.

7. *Privileged Questions.*—Privileged questions are those which take precedence of the business regularly before the house. They are:

(*a.*) To adjourn.

(*b.*) For the previous question.

(*c.*) For postponement.

(*d.*) For commitment.

(*e.*) For amendment.

(*f.*) To lie on the table.

A motion for postponement precludes commitment, and a motion for commitment precludes amendment.

8. *Personalities.*—The President may speak in his place to matters of order, or state facts which the members have occasion for. When he rises to speak the member occupying the floor should resume his seat. When a member is speaking, no conversation nor whispering should be indulged in, nor should any one pass between the speaker and the presiding officer. The decision of the President should always be submitted to quietly unless appealed from. A member decided to be out of order loses his right to the floor, without the unanimous consent of the house. No member when speaking should be interrupted, except by a call to order, or a proffer to explain. Members in debate should not refer to the other by name, but as the member who preceded me, last up, on the right, on the left, who opened the debate, etc. No member can be allowed to read an argument, or a paper pertaining to the discussion without unanimous consent. No member can address the house while sitting without unanimous consent. Any member rising to speak should address the President, and not proceed to speak until the President recognizes his right to the floor by announcing his name. When two or more members arise to speak at the same time, the President shall decide who is entitled to the floor by announcing his name, or designating him in some other manner. The motives of members are never to be questioned.

9. *Appeals.*—Any member may appeal from any decision of the Chair; but the member appealing must reduce his appeal to writing, and hand it to the Secretary. The President shall then state the question, and call for

a vote on the question, "Shall the decision of the Chair be sustained?"

10. *Explanations.*—No explanation can be made while a member is speaking without the consent of the speaker; but if the speaker yields the floor for an explanation, he cannot resume it again without unanimous consent. Members who obtain leave to explain must confine their remarks to the matters to be explained.

Committees.—In legislative bodies, committees are of two kinds, select or special, and standing or permanent. In Lyceums all committees are of the former kind. Their duties are to consider any subject or proposition referred to them, and report the same to the next meeting, or at any time designated. They may report in full or ask to be discharged, or report progress and ask leave to be continued. Their report may be considered and disposed of as a whole, or in sections or parts, when the subject is susceptible of such division. In the latter case each section may be approved, rejected, or amended, and then the final vote taken, whether it shall be adopted or rejected as a whole. The first person named on a committee of several usually acts as chairman.

11. *Postponements.*—These may be for the time, or indefinitely. When different times are mentioned the question should be taken on the most distant time first. The motion to postpone indefinitely cannot be amended, nor superseded by any other motion; but if decided negatively, a motion to amend or commit will be in order.

12. *Adjournment.*—A motion to adjourn is not in order when a member is speaking, nor when a vote is being taken on any question. When a motion to adjourn has been negatived, it cannot be renewed until some other

proposition has been presented, or business of some kind transacted. A motion to adjourn cannot be amended by adding to it a definite time or place; this must be previously decided on its own merits. A motion to adjourn to a particular time and place is debatable so far as the time and place are concerned. When desiring to suspend business temporarily, an adjournment for the time is in order, after which the business may be resumed on a simple motion to do so. When an adjournment has been voted during the consideration of any question, that question will be first put in order among the unfinished business, but not the first business in order at the next meeting.

CHAPTER IX.

The following questions are submitted for emergencies —when for want of time or for some other reason, the Lyceum is unable to agree on any question presented by the members.

Can a law of nature be suspended?

Ought the elective franchise to be extended to woman?

Are the sexes equal in mentality?

Is the female organization naturally more frail than that of the male?

Should public libraries be opened on Sunday?

Are schools or churches the greater benefit to society?

Is there more pleasure in pursuit than in possession?

Should immigration to this country be restricted?

Should eight hours be recognized as a legal day's work?

Resolved, that the veto power of the President be repealed.

Resolved, that all punishment should be limited to the reformation of the criminal.

Resolved, that capital punishment should be abolished.

Resolved, that all laws relating to interest on money should be repealed.

Resolved, that interest on money should be limited to the profits of productive industry.

Resolved, that all laws for the collection of debts should be repealed.

Resolved, that the rate of taxation should have reference to the property of the person taxed.

Resolved, that we suffer more from imaginary than from real evils.

Has the human race descended from a single pair?

Resolved, that conscience is an infallible rule for action.

Is the medical profession more useful than injurious?

Should national holidays be abolished?

Should the sexes be educated in the same schools?

Does geology harmonize with the Bible?

Should education be compulsory?

Is woman physiologically the " weaker vessel ? "

Does civilization progress more rapidly than the churches?

Is the theory of Darwin, as to the " descent of man," sustained by scientific data?

Is the doctrine of " Evolution " taught in the Bible?

Should white and colored children attend the same school?

Should society permit the existence of dram-shops?

Are alcoholic drinks a greater evil than tobacco?

Is the dietetic character of man frugivorous?

Is common salt useful as a condiment?

Should the property of churches be taxed?

Do labor-saving inventions benefit the laboring classes?

Are trades-unions justifiable?

Do great crises produce great men?

Ought old bachelors to be subject to civil disabilities?

Should monopolies in trade be allowed?

Ought ministers of the Gospel to engage in party politics?

Ought there to be a law of international copyright?

Is universal suffrage expedient?

Can the immortality of the soul be proved from the light of nature?

Do riches develop character better than poverty?

Is Roman Catholicism compatible with free institutions?

Ought imprisonment for debt to be abolished?

Is infidelity on the increase?

Is Phrenology a true science?

Is the assassination of tyrants justifiable?

Ought lotteries to be tolerated?

Are religious fairs justifiable?

Are ghosts the spirits of the departed?

Is youth a more happy period of life than old age?

Do preachers exercise a greater influence on the character of the young than teachers?

Are lawyers more beneficial than injurious to society?

Are women more revengeful than men?

Ought persons to marry who differ radically in religious opinions?

Are "all men created equal?"

Is the doctrine of original sin taught in the Bible?

Is morality separable from religion?

Does morality improve as civilization advances?

Is a Republic the best form of government?

Is the character of a nation affected by its climate?

Ought witnesses to be held as prisoners?

Is a declaration of war ever justifiable?

Resolved, that Satan is the hero of "Paradise Lost."

Is there such a quality as disinterestedness.

Ought patent-rights to be granted?

Does wealth exert more influence than knowledge?

Are banks more beneficial than injurious to a community?

Is there any real danger of over-population?

Are national celebrations beneficial?

Are persons accountable for their opinions?

Is man a free agent?

Are tea and coffee, as beverages, injurious?

Is it hygienic to drink at meals?

Is there more happiness than misery in human life?

Should the Bible be introduced into the common schools?

Is a falsehood ever justifiable?

Is the doctrine of non-resistance sound?

Resolved, that differences of character are attributable more to physical than to moral causes.

Is the slanderer a more pernicious character than the flatterer?

Do the phenomena of nature indicate polytheism?

Are ideas innate?

Ought emulation in schools to be encouraged?

Is corporeal punishment in schools justifiable?

Is rotation in office a correct principle?

Is it ever right to marry for money?

Is it expedient to wear mourning apparel?

Are graveyards expedient?

Would the practice of cremation be beneficial?

Is the miser more selfish than the profligate?

Ought one ever to advocate what he believes to be false?

Does proselytism favor the cause of truth?

Is the drunkard accountable for his conduct while drunk?

Do the Scriptures predict a millenium?

CPSIA information can be obtained
at www.ICGtesting.com
Printed in the USA
BVOW06*2001010817

490861BV00007B/46/P